The Early Pioneers of Las Vegas

Jeffrey A. Alpert

Designed by Thomas Messenger

Copyright © 2022 Jeffrey Alpert

All Rights Reserved

No portion of this book may be reproduced in any form or by any means without permission in writing from the author.

For all general information, please contact:

Jeffrey A. Alpert

Email: jalpert8@gmail.com

ISBN: 979-8-88526-982-7

On the cover:
Top Left - May 1905 photo of early stores on the west side of Main Street near Fremont Street
Top Right - Mayor and Businessman W.E. Hawkins
Mid Upper Left - Hotel Nevada at the southeast corner of Fremont and Main Streets in 1906
Mid Upper Right - Thomas' Department Store at the southwest corner of Fremont and 1st Streets
Mid Lower Left - The Thomas Block building on the northwest corner of Fremont and Main Streets
Mid Lower Right - The Block & Botkin clothing store on Fremont Street between 1st and 2nd Streets; 1905 photo
Bottom Left - Builder and businessman E.W. Griffith
Bottom Right - The Overland Hotel at the northeast corner of Fremont and Main Streets; circa 1910

DISCLAIMER:
The statements, opinions and photos contained in this publication are solely sourced, and provided by, the author and not the publisher or designer. The publisher and designer disclaims responsibility and liability for use of any and all material provided.

Introduction

The city of Las Vegas receives millions of visitors a year. They come to enjoy gambling, shows, sporting events, fine food and all the nice amenities the luxurious hotels have to offer. It is a most popular worldwide traveling destination.

Like many other American cities, Las Vegas came to be what it is today thanks to the railroad industry. Trains connected the area to major cities in other states, allowing for trade and development. With business opportunities came growth. Little attention is given to many of the early pioneers despite the risks they took. Few are probably household names. Yet they came to build a new life in the middle of a rough and tough desert. In this book, many of those original brave souls will be remembered for their contributions to early Las Vegas. For some of them, their chapter in this book will be the first time anything substantial has ever been written about them.

To prepare for this book I spent many hundreds of hours exploring the internet, libraries, microfilm, museums, books, ancestry websites and newspaper data bases. Many weeks were spent browsing through all the early editions of the Las Vegas Times and Las Vegas Age newspapers. Those early newspapers were very different than those of today. Much attention was given to local social activities (clubs, plays, operas, lodge activities, weddings, parades, etc.). If you were ill, it probably made it into the newspaper. Many articles covered mining news, roads, railroads, artesian wells, nearby ranches, and politics. When a local resident left town for pleasure or business, you could read about it.

Putting this book together was challenging but fun. Much was learned about how Las Vegas got its start and who some of the lesser-known players were. The motivation for writing about early Las Vegas pioneers came while writing my first two books. One was on the history of Kiel Ranch, a very historic place in North Las Vegas. The other was on the history of North Las Vegas and all of its mayors. Research for those books resulted in my being exposed to some of the early Las Vegas pioneers. I believe they deserve recognition for what they were able to accomplish, often under adverse conditions. We may live in the "present", but we should never fail to appreciate the "past".

Many references will be made to the early streets of Las Vegas. On the next page you will find a general map to assist in placing stores and buildings as you read about them. Today, the Fremont Street Experience light show canopy runs on Fremont from Main to 4th Street. The present-day name for 2nd Street is Casino Center Blvd. and 5th Street has become Las Vegas Blvd. North. Current casino names have been placed on the map as well so you may do then and now comparisons.

I hope you enjoy my third book.

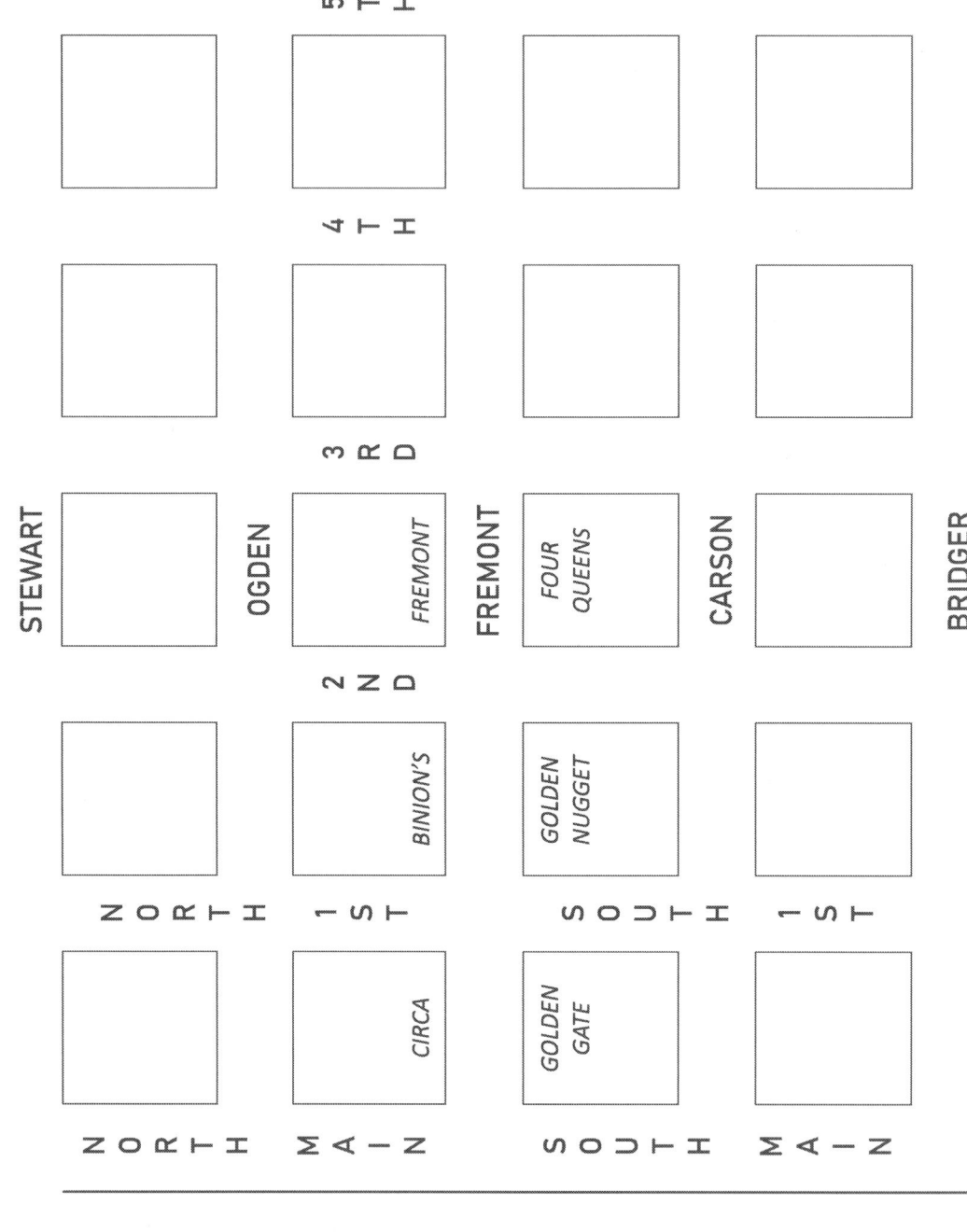

Acknowledgements

Researching and then writing this book was an intense and challenging eighteen-month project while Las Vegas was experiencing the horrible Covid virus. Many people were helpful along the way.

Crystal Van Dee and Sarah Hulme at the Nevada State Museum in Las Vegas were kind in their assistance. They guided me through use of the museum's microfilm, manuscript, and photo collections.

Su Kim Chung and her fine staff at the UNLV Libraries, Special Collection research facility were instrumental in giving me access to many remarkable manuscript and photo collections.

The Clark County Museum in Henderson, Nevada was able to supply me many useful photos. They also had a very nice early map collection. The museum is also home to the Beckley house which had photos and history on display.

I was able to make contact with Nancy Kramer Bryant who lives in Mesquite, Nevada. Her grandfather, Adam Kramer, was one of the first barbers in Las Vegas. She was very kind in sharing family history and photos.

Larry Gragg, a professor at the Missouri University of Science and Technology, has done extensive research on a variety of Las Vegas related topics. He was nice enough to direct me to his works that had significance to my investigations.

The Maple Hill Historical Society in Ohio was able to provide me with early information on Walter Bracken who was born in their town. Their shared material was excellent and pointed me in the direction of other resources as well.

Two local historians, Lisa Messenger and Robert Stoldal, share the same passion I have for early Las Vegas history. We support each other's interests and often share our findings. I thank them for their encouragement and shared knowledge. Robert was graciouos enough to review and comment on this book and then composed its foreword.

Finally, a big thank you to Lisa's husband Thomas Messenger. He helped organize my first two books and once again came through with this, my latest work. Without his assistance, this book would not have been printed.

Foreword

This book results from countless hours, days, weeks, and months of researching, digging deep, cross-checking, and finding both facts and images.

The result is a book packed with new details about the early days of Las Vegas.

Jeff combined research of the facts and the study of the visual images of the people and places found in this book.

While it is a collection of biographies of early settlers of Las Vegas, it is a series of stories about what it takes to build and sustain a new community.

And, it is also the story of the beginning of the hospitality industry in Las Vegas, along with bankers, builders, and barbers.

This book is Jeff's third as he continues to preserve the history of southern Nevada by bringing it to life and making it available for all to enjoy.

After reading and enjoying Jeff's first books on southern Nevada and understanding his passion and dedication to expanding the knowledge of our communities, "The Early Pioneers of Las Vegas" is a must-read for anyone interested in southern Nevada, Clark County, and Las Vegas.

Robert Stoldal
Student of Nevada History

Table of Contents

CHAPTER 1: The Birth of a Town ....Page 1

CHAPTER 2: Colonel Ladd ....Page 7

CHAPTER 3: Norman Kuhn ....Page 15

CHAPTER 4: William Thomas ....Page 21

CHAPTER 5: The Kramer Brothers ....Page 29

CHAPTER 6: The Boggs Brothers ....Page 37

CHAPTER 7: Ivan Botkin ....Page 43

CHAPTER 8: John Wisner and the Overland Hotel ....Page 47

CHAPTER 9: John Miller and the Hotel Nevada ....Page 59

CHAPTER 10: Jake and Will Beckley ....Page 69

CHAPTER 11: Walter Bracken ....Page 81

CHAPTER 12: Moyd Thomas ....Page 87

CHAPTER 13: E.W. Griffith ....Page 95

CHAPTER 14: William Hawkins ....Page 103

CHAPTER 15: Dr. Roy Martin ....Page 111

CHAPTER 16: William Ferron ....Page 123

CHAPTER 17: Scammers, Schemers and Dreamers ....Page 133

Chapter 1
The Birth of a Town

The Las Vegas Valley in 1900 looked absolutely nothing like it does today. There were no paved roads, no stores, no utilities, no housing communities, no cars, no large hotels and casinos, and very few residents. The 1900 Federal Census listed only 11 adults, 2 children, and 5 servants in the Las Vegas Precinct. On its far-off outskirts there were some 250 folks living mainly in the scattered mining districts of Eldorado Canyon, Searchlight, Crescent, Sandy and Goodsprings. Life was definitely not easy.

Mormon missionaries from Utah had established a fort settlement in "Los Vegas" in the mid-1800's that only lasted about two years. The area was chosen as it was about midway along the winding Mormon Trail that connected Salt Lake City and Southern California. The region had a good supply of water and the soil was suitable for crops. Octavius Decatur Gass took over the abandoned fort in the mid-1860's but when he failed to meet a loan payment deadline in the early 1880's he was forced to leave the property. Archibald and Helen Stewart of Pioche, the holders of his loan, decided to occupy the ranch after Gass vacated it. When Archibald was mysteriously murdered on the nearby Kiel Ranch in 1884, a brave Helen took over the operation of the property as she reared her many children. She had a wonderful relationship with the local Paiute Indians and over time greatly expanded her land holdings in the region.

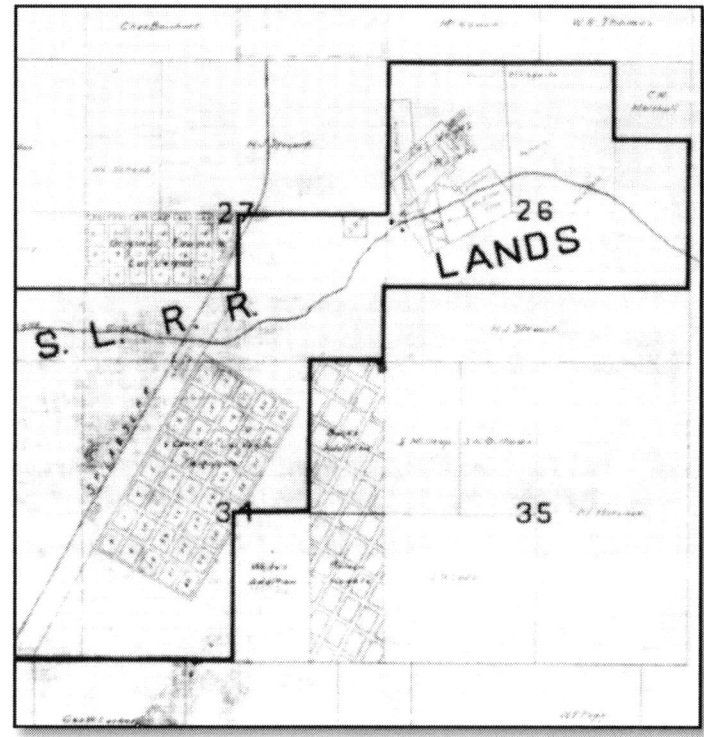

The outlined area shows part of the land the railroad purchased. Their new town of Las Vegas is located on a diagonal in the middle left with the Stewart Ranch in the upper right. This map of land holdings was created by surveyor J.T. McWilliams in May of 1905. McWilliams had started his own town which can be seen in the top left section of this map.
UNLV Libraries, Special Collections

Soon after 1900, wealthy copper baron and powerful Montana U.S. Senator William A. Clark had desires to build a railroad (mainly to transfer ore from his mines) that would connect Salt Lake City and Los Angeles' port at San Pedro. He owned numerous mines, mills, smelters, banks, newspapers, and railroads. Clark organized the San Pedro, Los Angeles and Salt Lake Railroad Company (SP-LA-SL). A rival, E. H. Harriman, who owned the Union Pacific Railroad had the same idea. Harriman already owned numerous rights-of-way under his Oregon Short Line subsidiary. The race was on.

As conflicts arose, both Clark and Harriman came to realize that it would be advantageous if they formed a partnership. Two competing nearly parallel lines would not be wise or profitable. Harriman became a 50% partner in the SP-LA-SL Railroad in 1903. A mid-way "division" point would be needed that could house required railroad facilities. Scouts had been dispatched in 1901 to locate such a place. They found that the Las Vegas area would be a practical spot to meet the railroad's needs. Railroad interests purchased the Kiel Ranch in July of 1901 and then Helen Stewart's vast holdings (including water rights) shortly thereafter.

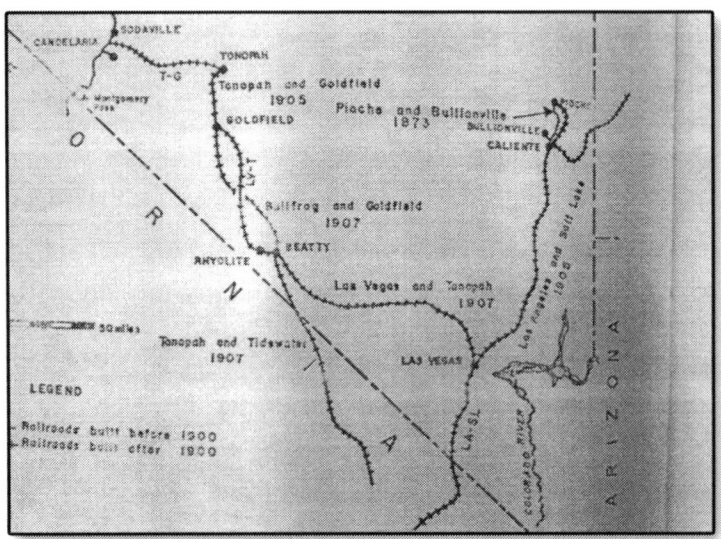

The LA-SL route from California to Utah as it winds its way through Nevada is shown vertically on the right

The tracks from Salt Lake City to Las Vegas were completed in October of 1904 followed by the leg from Los Angeles to Las Vegas in late January of 1905.

The SP-LA-SL Railroad made plans to lay out a townsite on the east side of their tracks, not far from the Stewart Ranch. A subsidiary called the Las Vegas Land and Water Co. was organized. It would control land and water in the region as well as the new proposed townsite. The railroad would be involved in most land, water, and civic issues in Las Vegas for decades to come.

As the railroad executives negotiated to buy land, they were smart to include the "Big Springs" location in their purchase (today the site of the Las Vegas Springs Preserve). It was the source of the water that flowed in the creek towards and through Stewart's ranch. It was about 40 feet wide.

Both Stewart and the railroad used experienced local surveyor and civil engineer J.T. McWilliams to study and prepare reports on the lands involved. When McWilliams became privy to the plans of the railroad for a townsite, he smartly did his own purchase from Helen of some 80 acres that she had not included in the negotiations. His goal was to beat the railroad and establish his own townsite on the west side of the tracks. He quickly developed his plat map and successfully filed it with Lincoln County before the end of 1904.

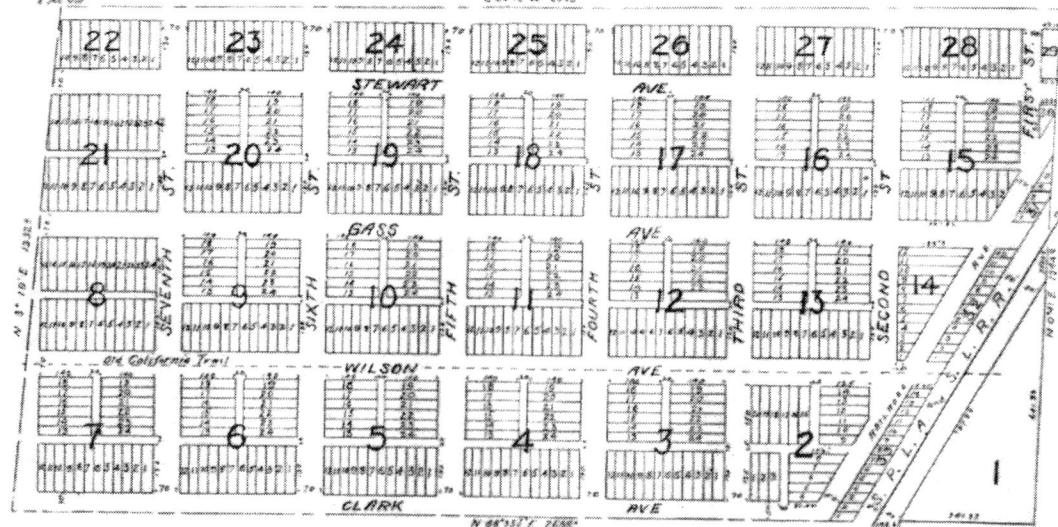

Plat map of "McWilliams' Original Las Vegas Townsite"
UNLV Libraries, Special Collections

He began advertising his lots in Los Angeles newspapers. By the early months of 1905, his lots were being quickly purchased. Seven saloons, a restaurant and a general store soon opened.

McWilliams' new town had to depend on numerous small wells. He did not have access to the railroad's creek water. Building materials were very scarce so the homes and stores that went up were made of a combination of wood and canvass. They had the appearance of a cloth tent which lead to his community getting the name "Ragtown". Nonetheless, his town expanded rapidly with most of the residents being teamsters involved with the transportation of goods to regional mining camps.

The executives of the SP-LA-SL Railroad obviously were not happy with the jump McWilliams had on their town. However, they knew they could market their town more successfully as it would be adjacent to the soon-to-be-built train depot and have a good supply of readily available water. Furthermore, merchants would be pleased with the hundreds of local railroad employees who had payroll checks to spend. They were correct. When their town did get started in May of 1905 there was a quick mass exodus of residents and stores from McWilliams' townsite which then declined quickly. What remained of his inferior town was seriously destroyed by a fire on September 5, 1905. Some remaining folks would rebuild but McWilliams' townsite forever stood in the shadow of the more successful Clark Townsite. McWilliams' town would become known as "Old Town" and later on turned into the segregated community of Las Vegas called "West Las Vegas" or simply the "Westside".

A dejected J.T. McWilliams left for his home country of Canada for a few years. Most of his lot buyers had only made a small down payment and many walked away without paying off their balances. Instead of being a wealthy land developer, he was stuck with many unpaid bills.

Now let's turn our attention to see how Clark's Townsite actually got started. Again, with McWilliams beating them to the punch in filing his plat and the selling of lots, railroad executives were extremely anxious to move their planning along rapidly. They were able to produce a tentative plat map before the end of February of 1905.

The town would have 38 "blocks" with most of them subdivided into 32 lots each. Streets were named from Main to 5th going west to east, and Stewart to Garces going north to south. Blocks 1, 2 and 3 near the planned-for train depot would have different sized lots to better accommodate businesses. Lots in the other blocks would have standard sizes of 25 feet by 140 feet. Alleys twenty feet wide would run through the blocks and roads would be 80 feet in width. All blocks were 300 feet by 400 feet in dimensions. Block 18 was reserved for a town library and courthouse. Only establishments in blocks 16 and 17 would be allowed to sell alcohol.

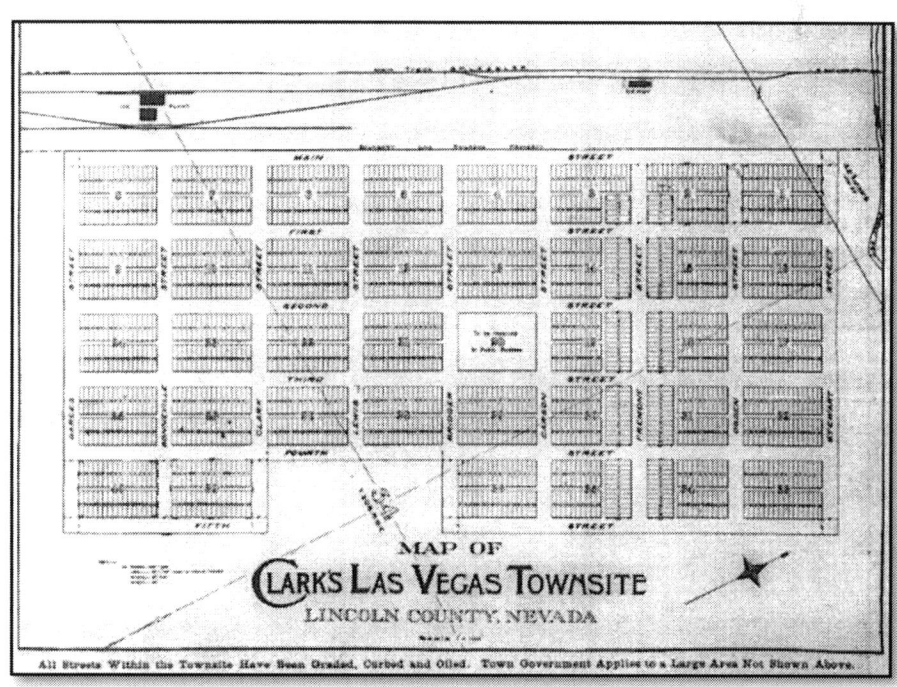

1905 plat map of "Clark's Las Vegas Townsite"
UNLV Libraries, Special Collections

A railroad committee asked soon-to-be First State Bank cashier John S. Park to begin taking applications from potential lot buyers in April of 1905. The railroad had already begun advertising their new town in Los Angeles and Salt Lake City newspapers. When they saw how much interest was being generated, the executives directed Park to notify all the applicants that the sale of the lots would be switching to an auction. Their goal was "to get all the money they could out of the townsite." Park had just a few days to notify those who placed applications to buy lots that an auction would be upcoming. Applications already submitted were destroyed.

Day one of the proposed two-day lot auction commenced on May 15, 1905. An auctioneer's stand had been erected at the intersection of Main and Ogden. Unfortunately, the first day turned out to be a brutally hot one of 110 degrees. Estimations of the size of the enthusiastic crowd of bidders varied from hundreds to thousands. Most were from coastal Los Angeles and were not properly dressed for such a torrid day. The new town had no shade trees so many struggled with the heat as the auction went forward.

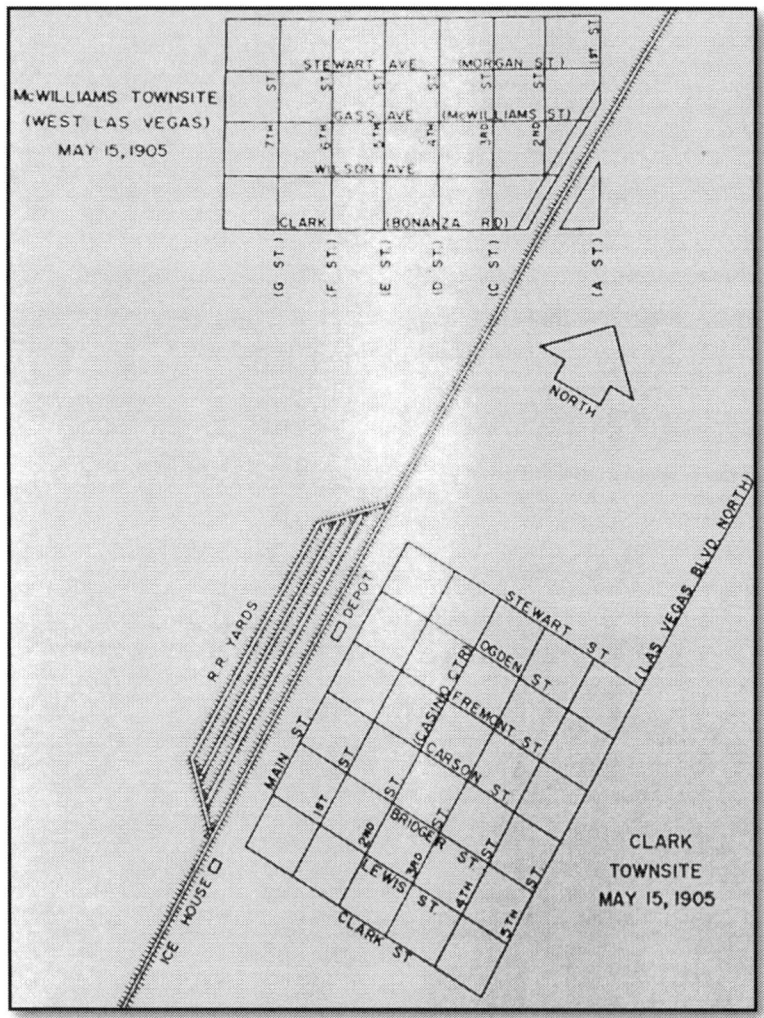

The railroad's townsite is shown in this map on the bottom and McWilliams' Original Townsite on the top. The map also shows in parentheses future street name changes that came about

Those arriving from Los Angeles had paid $16 for a round-trip train ticket and the cost from Salt Lake City was a bit higher at $20. The railroad promised a full refund to any buyer who paid for a purchased lot in full. Opening bid amounts were set by the railroad committee. Successful bidders had the option of putting $25 down with 60 days to pay off the balance, after which the process to get them their deed would commence.

Not all lots on all blocks went on the market. Some blocks had yet to be fully surveyed with lots staked off by wooden sticks. Many a successful buyer had trouble locating their lot(s) due to how dusty the town was. On May 15 some 176 lots were auctioned off and brought in $77,566. California bidders drove up prices, especially for prime business lots near the proposed depot. The railroad decided that on May 16 the remaining (less desirable) lots would be sold at fixed prices. That went over well and generated an additional $265,000 in sales with close to half the lots still available purchased.

With initial sales completed, many buyers were anxious to get their homes and businesses going despite the hot and dusty conditions. Those from McWilliams' townsite who bought lots quickly disassembled their tent homes to move to the new town and put their businesses on rollers to transport over. Again, proper building supplies were very limited, so the first homes and businesses were again structures of wood and canvass. Brick buildings would soon follow.

It took brave men to take a chance on a new life in a brand-new town in a very remote and barren region. Most of them would wait until the fall or winter when the weather improved to send for their families. This book is dedicated to those courageous early pioneers who threw caution to the wind to start a new life in the area we now know as Downtown Las Vegas. Great effort was taken to accurately research and tell their stories.

Chapter 2
Colonel James H. Ladd
Hotelier, Businessman and Developer

One of the earliest men to arrive in Las Vegas was an elderly but colorful character by the name of Colonel James Henry Ladd, or just Colonel Jim Ladd as the locals would refer to him. He also liked to go by Captain Ladd as well. He was a Civil War veteran.

James Ladd was born on June 5, 1841, in Galena, Illinois. His father was a grocer. When the Civil War broke out, James enlisted and would fight for the North with the Indiana Infantry. He rose to the rank of Colonel. After the war ended, Jim roamed the country as he made his way west. He loved to gamble and even tried his hand at mining. In the early 1870's he spent time in the Montana Territory before moving on to reside in Tombstone, Arizona along with other rough and rugged small towns in the area. Later in life he would boast how in 1881 he had visited the desolate region where the Boulder Dam would be built some fifty years later.

A 1900 photo of James Ladd

In the 1880's James was a saloon keeper in San Bernardino, California. When a gold rush up in the Northwest started in the late 1890's, James was off to the Yukon Territory. He participated in the Klondike Gold Rush and lived for a while in Nome, Alaska where he operated a gaming establishment.

A railroad car was used as a temporary depot
UNLV Libraries, Special Collections

By late 1904 (at the age of 63) James found his way to Las Vegas where the railroad would soon complete a line stretching from Southern California all the way to Salt Lake City in Utah. In January of 1905 he purchased a lot for $125 in J.T. McWilliams' Townsite, but it is not known what he did with it. Perhaps he set up a tent home there. Realizing the need for lodging for railroad employees and early visitors to the windy and dusty area (arriving by team from California and Utah or by railroad construction cabooses), Ladd established the first hotel in Las Vegas. It was a white tent structure some 16 feet by 20 feet which he located with the permission of the railroad near the temporary train depot adjacent to Main Street, close to Carson Street.

His hotel had a small lobby at the front entrance and just two bedrooms set up in the rear. Each bedroom had two double beds. A small area of the tent was available for bathing and shaving. With no other lodging available other than on the Stewart Ranch, Ladd rented out his in-demand beds in eight-hour shifts. Folks would pay 50 cents each (payable in advance) to share a bed with a stranger. One was not allowed to rent a whole bed for himself. He accepted his first guest on February 13, 1905, some three months before the railroad would auction off town lots.

Cover of hotel ledger book used by Colonel Ladd. The register survived and is housed at *UNLV Libraries, Special Collections*

Many of the early Las Vegas pioneers being written about in this book were guests of Ladd's Hotel. Early newspaper editor "Pop" Squires who stayed in the tent hotel would recall many decades later how Ladd was a no-nonsense type of guy. When strangers would show up to rent one of his beds, he would announce that he was all booked up (when he wasn't) but stated that they could hang around for a vacancy to occur. After observing them for a while, if he saw they did not continuously scratch themselves, he would approach and offer them a bed. Ladd's rules were the "law". Once, a guest had complained of a leak in the roof above his bed. An upset Ladd charged him extra to take a bath.

After the railroad's auction of lots, many newly arriving lot owners put up their own temporary tents for lodging. Numerous wooden structures were built which included primitive hotels. There was no longer a need for Ladd's tent hotel, so the railroad asked him to take it down at the end of May, 1905. James saw the potential of the new little town in the desert. He bought some lots from the railroad at the auction as well homesteaded 160 acres in 1906 of land along Fremont Street about a mile or so beyond the end of railroad's eastern town boundary.

Wooden structure on 3rd Street that housed Ladd's lodging facility.

In June of 1905, with his tent now gone just months after opening, James would build a wooden hotel structure (first called "Hotel Del Plaza" or "Plaza House") on his property opposite Block 19 (which was not sold by the railroad so it could serve as a community plaza). Ladd's rooming house was on South 3rd Street.

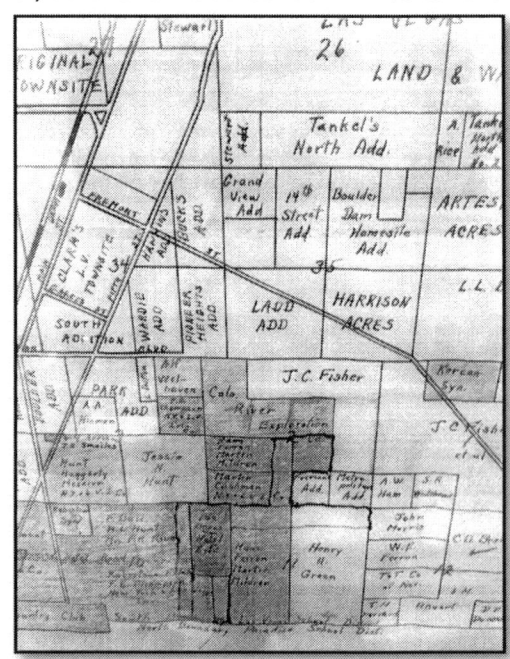

A 1936 map showing the Ladd Addition in the center of the map. *Courtesy of the Clark County Museum*

His facility started off small and attracted prominent early Las Vegas pioneers such as Walter Bracken and businessman W.E. Hawkins. In early 1907 Ladd purchased two wooden buildings in town and moved them next to his business now called "Plaza Hotel" to form a courtyard complex which would eventually have ferns, palms, and potted plants. On Sunday's bands would play music and his guests were treated to sandwiches and cold beverages. His operation grew to 18 furnished rooms that were available for daily, weekly or monthly rental.

On his Fremont land east of town Ladd planted hundreds of shade trees and started a grape vineyard. He found the soil to be "deep and mellow". He would lease some of the land for dairy ranching and a poultry business when he saw that his supply of surface water was dwindling. Neither made a go of it. Spring-fed surface water was insufficient and one of the proprietors passed away. Ladd returned to his property, drilled a well, and would try his own hand at farming. He had a good enough flow of water to form a reservoir. He made fence posts from Moapa cottonwoods and used tightly strung barbed-wire.

Colonel Ladd became the local agent for a stage line that ran carriages between Las Vegas and Beatty. He once bragged that he rode a carriage by himself some 70 miles in just 6 hours. It is documented that he purchased a wagon, horses, and accessories from the railroad in 1905 when some of the Old Stewart Ranch inventory was being liquidated.

James Ladd is standing by his stagecoach on the far right in this photo circa 1906 taken in the now Boulder City area
UNLV Libraries, Special Collections

A 1910 photo of folks posing by Ladd's stagecoach in the old Las Vegas Wash
UNLV Libraries, Special Collections

Ladd's stagecoach makes its way along a rugged trail in this 1911 photo taken in the Ft. Callville, Nevada region
UNLV Libraries, Special Collections

James loved to gamble and he would often frequent the Arizona Club on North 1st Street.

Colonel Ladd is seen in a hat facing the camera on the far end of the gambling table inside the Arizona Club in this photo circa 1906
UNLV Libraries, Special Collections

Another photo inside the Arizona Club circa 1910. Ladd is front center in the white hat

In June of 1906 he and local businessman B.F. Boggs established a mining claim in the Vincent District that looked promising. In late 1907 he partnered with businessman and contractor E.W. Griffith to buy property and water rights in the "Whispering Ben Creek" region, about ten miles west of Indian Creek. He would also partner with others to pursue mining interests just outside of town. He dabbled in lumber interests as well and would contract to sink artesian wells in and out of town.

In early 1911 Ladd began surveying his land along Fremont Street between 11th and 14th Streets. He created a subdivision of 40 acres and began selling lots for $50 each. Customers would only pay $5 up front and then could pay off the rest in nine monthly payments of $5 each. Corner lots went for $75. It did not take him long to sell his first 50 lots.

February 25, 1911, Las Vegas Age ad

Undated ad for Ladd's Resort pool

He began construction of an amusement hall and the town's first public swimming pool or "plunge" as it was referred to (at Fremont and 12th) using his well water.

Early photo circa 1911 showing people
enjoying the pool after it first opened
UNLV Libraries, Special Collections

Folks enjoying Ladd's resort pool circa 1910's
UNLV Libraries, Special Collections

Photo circa 1910's showing Ladd's pool
UNLV Libraries, Special Collections

Undated photo of Colonel Ladd (far right)
with guests at his pool
Courtesy of Nevada State Museum, Las Vegas

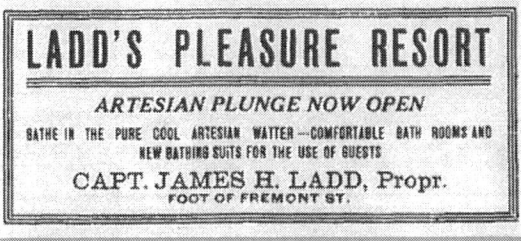

July 1, 1911, Las Vegas Age ad for
Ladd's Pleasure Resort

Ladd started making arrangements to sink more wells on his property so homes could have water and his pool could be kept filled. By late April 1911 construction was underway on a 30 by 60 foot concrete dancing pavilion adjacent to the pool as well as 10 private bath houses for private changing into swimming attire. He drew up plans to add a restaurant and a 24 by 40 foot saloon. "Ladd's Pleasure Resort" opened on June 8, 1911, with a 4-piece orchestra on hand and bus service provided to and from the nearby town. His timing was good as the pool was very popular and extremely busy that summer. By 1913 the city was ready to grade and connect Fremont Street out to Ladd's area and beyond.

While Ladd developed his subdivision, he continued to run his Plaza House on South 3rd Street.

January 4, 1908, Las Vegas Age ad

The new courthouse was constructed on Block 19 adjacent to the much smaller old one seen on the left in this photo taken circa 1914

Clark County completed a large $57,000 courthouse on the Plaza across from his lodging house in November of 1914.

Unfortunately, not long thereafter a fire destroyed Ladd's hotel structures and he decided not to rebuild. He continued to focus his attention on his subdivision along with his Pleasure Resort (which was on the south side of Fremont between 11th and what is now Maryland Parkway).

In 1915 James planted many cottonwoods on his subdivision and brought in carloads of pipe to disperse water from his wells. A November 1915 fire destroyed his dancing pavilion resulting in $2500 worth of damage. Six months later he had rebuilt the pavilion and it now included a popular skating rink.

An August 1919 article in the local newspaper mentioned that Ladd was filing for divorce from an A.L.J. Clark. Nothing is really known about his married life. His death certificate would make mention of a wife by the name of May Ladd. He never had any known children.

Colonel Ladd also owned land in Pahrump and in 1922 he dug a well on his "Wheat Fields" property. He knew the well would make his land more valuable. By that time there were some 15 families living in the area near Sandy.

During the 1920's Ladd added rental cabins to his resort creating an auto court and remodeled the dancing pavilion. In July of 1930 at age 89 the Colonel fell critically ill from heart failure complications. He was hospitalized but recovered. After recuperating at home, he went to Los Angeles where he fell ill again but again survived.

In October of 1930 the only other Civil War veteran in the area passed away leaving James as the last one within Clark County. Colonel Ladd participated in Las Vegas' 1931 Memorial Day parade, traveling down Fremont Street in a car and vigorously waving to viewers lining the route. That summer he opened up more lots for sale in his Ladd Addition (on both sides of Fremont near 14th Street).

Once again Ladd fell ill in December of 1932 and managed to recover. Still ambitious as a 91 year old man who didn't even need to wear glasses, he would open a bar and a blacksmith shop at Fremont and 11th Streets. Soon thereafter his health began to fail and he died at home of heart failure on January 13, 1934 at age 92.

LAST SURVIVOR OF CIVIL WAR IN COUNTY, DIES

Lingering Illness Is Fatal To Widely Known Resident; Was 92

Jim Ladd, Clark county's last known surviving civil war veteran, and one of the pioneers of the old west, passed away at 4:30 this morning at his home on Fremont street, near Fourteenth, after a lingering illness.

A portion of a Review Journal article from January 13, 1934, announcing Ladd's passing

Grave marker for Ladd in the Goodsprings Cemetery
Find-A-Grave Website

His survivors were four grandnephews. After a widely attended service in Las Vegas, the Colonel was buried in the Goodsprings Cemetery. Among his distinguished pallbearers were railroad agent Walter Bracken and J.T. McWilliams who founded the original Las Vegas townsite.

Colonel James H. Ladd had a long and adventurous life. He was a soldier, miner, gambler, hotelier, developer, and businessman; just one of many ambitious and interesting early Las Vegas pioneers!

Chapter 3
Norman A. Kuhn
merchant

Perhaps the first store merchant to open a business in the vicinity of the railroad's new townsite was Norman Alfred Kuhn. He did not remain in Las Vegas a long time like other pioneers, but his presence was extremely important in helping others get established. What little is known about him comes mostly from old U.S. Census information and newspaper articles. No photos of him or his family members could be discovered.

Norman's father was John Morgan Kuhn, a physician, who was born October 27, 1811, in Allegheny County, Pennsylvania. He attended Washington and Jefferson College in Cannonsburg, Pennsylvania and in 1836 obtained a degree from Franklin College in New Athens, Ohio. His desire was to become a minister, but when he lost his voice as the result of a bad fever, he turned to studying medicine. He received his medical certification from Jefferson Medical College in Philadelphia. Dr. Morgan moved to Eastern Ohio where he partnered with another doctor and lived on a large farm. In December of 1845 he married his partner's oldest daughter, Katherine Robertson, who was 17 years his junior. Together they would have six children -- Anna (1846), Maggie (1848), Norman (1854), Alice (1856), Catherine (1859) and Kittie (1860).

A drawing of the Kuhn family home in Omaha, Nebraska

Sometime in the 1850's the Kuhn family relocated to Omaha, Nebraska. There was a domestic and global financial panic in 1857 during which many struggled. Dr. Morgan in 1863 would up the family from Nebraska and move to Salem, Ohio where he would open a drugstore. He was a known supporter of the Underground Railway and often helped escaping slaves along their journey to Canada. Dr. Morgan was also one of the original organizers of the Republican Party. Around 1880, he relocated back to Omaha.

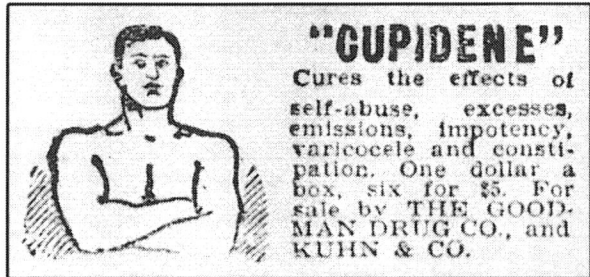
An ad from the May 30, 1895, Omaha Daily Bee newspaper for a "drug" available at Kuhn's store

He became an elder in the First Presbyterian Church there. He passed away at age 92 on May 5, 1903. His wife Katherine had died just two weeks before him.

Norman was raised by his parents in both Ohio and Nebraska. In spring of 1877 he graduated from the College of Pharmacology in Philadelphia, Pennsylvania. He returned to live in Omaha, Nebraska where he became a druggist like his father. In 1879 he started a drug store at the corner of 15th and Douglas Streets. By the end of 1881 he was doing an impressive $25,000 in annual sales.

In 1885 he was elected the president of the Nebraska State Pharmaceutical Association. During the summer of 1888 he fell severely ill and almost died. He recovered and later that year became a board member of the Nebraska Savings Bank.

Norman married Ella ("Helen") B. Preston in June of 1889 in Douglas, Nebraska. She was 13 years younger than him. They had two children.

In 1890 Norman received a permit to sell products in his store containing liquor. He dabbled in real estate and had multiple cottages for either sale or rent. In late 1890 he along with four partners started the Northwestern Investment Company.

Norman Kuhn employed and trained many local druggists over the years at his Omaha business. In 1902 he helped form the Wyoming Oil Company. After about a quarter of a century as a druggist, Norman decided in 1905 to quit the drug business and sold his store.

How and why, Norman wound up in Las Vegas in early 1905 at age 51 is not known. Perhaps it was his growing interest in mining opportunities in Southern Nevada. Norman's name first surfaced in Las Vegas when in early March of 1905 his name appeared on the registry of Colonel Jim Ladd's small tent hotel near the temporary train depot.

The railroads' general store while on the Old Stewart Ranch
UNLV Libraries, Special Collections

Prior to the arrival of the railroad, there were but a handful of people residing in the area. Helen Stewart sold her ranch and most of her land holdings in 1902 to Senator William A. Clark's railroad company. She had been residing there since 1882 and was the greater area's postmaster. The railroad took possession of all the structures on her "Old Ranch". They made plans to sell some of them as they prepared for the auction of their lots in their nearby new town. The railroad moved the ranch's general store in early February of 1905 to Main Street, adjacent to the temporary rail depot (where the Plaza Hotel sits today).

It began doing a brisk business with the railroad's workers and filled contracts for goods needed in outlying mining districts. Having just recently arrived in Las Vegas, Kuhn made a deal with the railroad's people in mid-March to buy the structure and all of its contents for about $6000. He opened up Kuhn's Mercantile and by early April was ready to sell groceries, hardware, miner tools, tents, boots, shoes, and general dry goods.

Ad in Las Vegas Age newspaper for Kuhn's Mercantile store

A busy day for Kuhn's store perhaps on the day the First State Bank opened in May of 1905. A portion of the town's first post office can be seen to the right of Kuhn's store in the photo. On the left was a Chinese restaurant that also came from the Old Ranch.
UNLV Libraries, Special Collections

April 28, 1905 ad for summer hats and shirts in the Las Vegas Times

Moving sale ad in the June 3, 1905 Las Vegas Age

Another Kuhn ad from July 15, 1905. He advertised regularly in both the Las Vegas Age and the Las Vegas Times newspapers.

June 24, 1905 Kuhn ad for his store now located near the southeast corner of Main and Fremont Streets

June 10, 1905, Las Vegas Age ad

Norman also planned to sell drugs. In early May of 1905, he allowed the directors of the First State Bank to open up a temporary bank in a corner of his store while they arranged to build a two-story wooden structure at the northeast corner of Fremont and 1st Streets.

Kuhn also leased out space in his store for an ice cream operation.

Norman had participated in the May land auction, purchasing three lots. He planned to bring his wife and two children to Las Vegas from Omaha after the hot summer ended.

As the young town started to quickly grow, Kuhn joined the Las Vegas Board of Trade and served as its president. Kuhn's Mercantile sat on railroad land which they needed for a permanent depot structure. His store was put on jacks and braced in early June for a move across Main Street, near the southeast corner with Fremont.

About two months later Norman had to move his store again when his corner was needed by J.F. Miller to build a hotel. He relocated around the corner into the new Fullmer & Herrick Building on north Fremont between Main and First Streets. Kuhn's Mercantile was now in a nice solid structure with pane glass windows.

Rare photo found in Volume 1 of the 1935 book "Nevada History". Kuhn occupied the middle of three stores.
Small print on his sign says Hardware, Boots, Clothing, Shoes, Gents Furnishing Goods, Drugs, Prospector's Outfits.

In the summer of 1905 Kuhn opened a second general store, this time in the area that was to become Nipton, California.

It was first known as Nippeno and was located 20 miles west of Searchlight. Kuhn had eager customers in the miners from surrounding encampments.

In late August of 1905 Norman went to the Portland, Oregon Exposition and reported that many Easterners were attending. In mid-November he was in Reno to receive certification as a pharmacist from the Nevada State Board of Pharmacies.

In January of 1906 the Las Vegas Age reported that Kuhn went to the Colorado River to inspect some of his mining properties. In April the sidewalk in front of his store on Fremont was cemented.

September 16, 1905, Kuhn ad indicating his two store locations

Another Age Kuhn ad, this one relating to mining

An April 21, 1906 Age Kuhn ad

Norman's wife and children spent the summer in Long Beach, California to escape the desert heat. Norman went to the east coast for three weeks to represent the Golden Triangle Mining & Development Co. of which he was president (the mines were southeast of Las Vegas). Upon his return to town, he was eager to tell all how good he found crops and businesses along his routes of travel.

In the Las Vegas Age of December 22, 1906, it was reported that the Kuhn family had recently moved to Los Angeles and that he would visit occasionally to check on his mines. It is not known what became of his store in town. Thus ended his shorter than two year stay in Las Vegas.

Norman did return in April of 1907 for a visit. The Age reported in September of 1907 that the Kuhn's were living in Edgecomb, Washington. Norman was operating a roof shingle mill that had 40 employees and was capable of turning out up to 125,000 shingles per day. Norman visited Las Vegas again in December of 1907 and said the lumber industry in the Puget Sound area of Washington was very quiet.

In March of 1908 it was reported that the Las Vegas Land and Water Company was suing Norman as he never finished paying for the lots he purchased in May of 1905. The 1910 U.S. Census had the Kuhn family still residing in Edgecomb; Norman was now 55 years old. While there he helped organize a club (The Omaha and Council Bluffs Club of Seattle) for the many residents who had relocated from the mid-west. It claimed over 100 members.

In March of 1912 it was reported Norman was frequenting the Hotel Fresno in San Francisco. In March of 1913 Kuhn visited Las Vegas, some six years after departing town. It was mentioned in the Age that he was in the real estate business in Sacramento, California. The 1920 Census had him living in Flournoy, California about 100 miles northwest of Sacramento. He and his son were listed as farmers and did ranching as well.

Norman's and Helen's last visit to Las Vegas was in June of 1925. He recalled a funny story from 1905 when he was advertising a pair of shoes for $1. A man with one amputated leg entered his store and wanted to buy two right shoes for a dollar.

Norman Kuhn would die on April 1, 1926, in California at age 72. The 1930 Census had Helen Kuhn living with her son Norman Jr. in Chico City, California. She would outlive Norman by about 25 years, passing away at age 88 in Sacramento, California.

Kuhn's Mercantile store was essential in helping Las Vegas get established. He sold shoes, clothing, mining supplies, tools, drugs, household goods, and food staples. Despite being in early Las Vegas for less than two years, Norman Alfred Kuhn will be remembered as the young railroad town's first general merchant. Quite a distinction.

Chapter 4
William Raymond Thomas
Lawyer, Judge, District Attorney, Builder, Community Activist

One of the early Las Vegas pioneers who played many important roles was William Raymond Thomas. His accomplishments during his 15 years in Las Vegas were staggering. He was an early builder, a lawyer, a judge, a district attorney, and a most civic-minded citizen.

William R. Thomas was born on October 13, 1855, in the city of Berlin, Wisconsin. He spent his youth on a farm before his family moved to Iowa. William graduated from the Des Moines School of Law in 1878 and moved to Watertown, South Dakota after obtaining his law degree. South Dakota was not yet a state and Watertown was a sizable town of about 6,000 residents. It was a railroad hub on the western edge of civilization in the area. Young William was able to land a job as the territory's registrar of deeds after arriving in 1878. Two years later he became president of the town's Board of Trade and in April of 1881 he was approved to practice law in South Dakota. William married Mary Peterson of Minnesota. An ambitious William went on to become city attorney and mayor of Watertown, president of the local school board, and vice-president of a town bank. In 1889 South Dakota became a state and William Thomas was elected as the first State Senator in his local district. He served one term in the legislature. He was a large land owner and in 1904 his family traveled through most of Europe for months.

A 1910 Masonic Lodge photo of William Thomas

William and wife Mary had three children while residing in Watertown -- Ralph, James and Marie. William suffered from asthma which may be the reason he relocated the family to the dryer and less humid desert climate of Southern Nevada. They arrived in Las Vegas in early 1905 with William already reaching the age of 49. On March 4, 1905, William was admitted to practice law in Nevada. He arrived with substantial funds and became a land speculator. In April 1905 he purchased a large 80 acre parcel about a mile northeast of the Old Stewart Ranch that he hoped to divide into 5 acre lots to sell.

Thomas was an active bidder on day one of the railroad's auction of town lots. Over the two days, William was successful in buying 16 choice lots -- one at the southwest corner of 1st and Ogden, two at the northwest corner on Fremont and 1st, two near the northwest corner of Fremont and 2nd, two at the southeast corner of Fremont and 1st, four at the southeast corner of Fremont and 2nd, four on

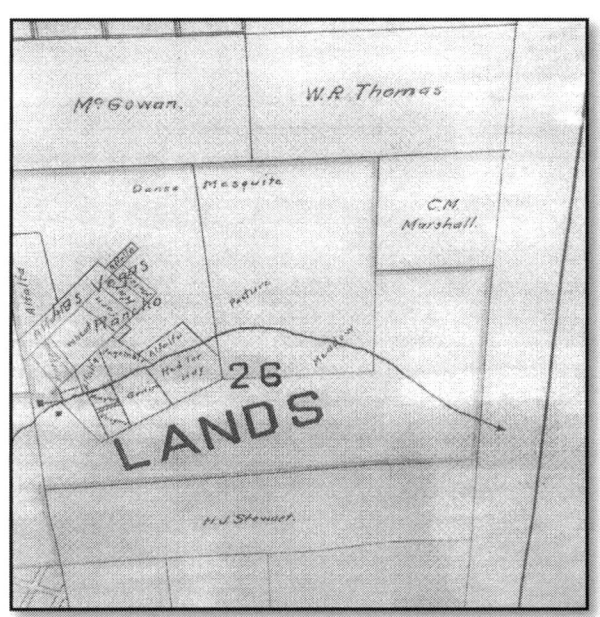
A map circa 1910 showing Thomas' plot of land about a mile away from the Old Ranch.
Courtesy of the Clark County Museum

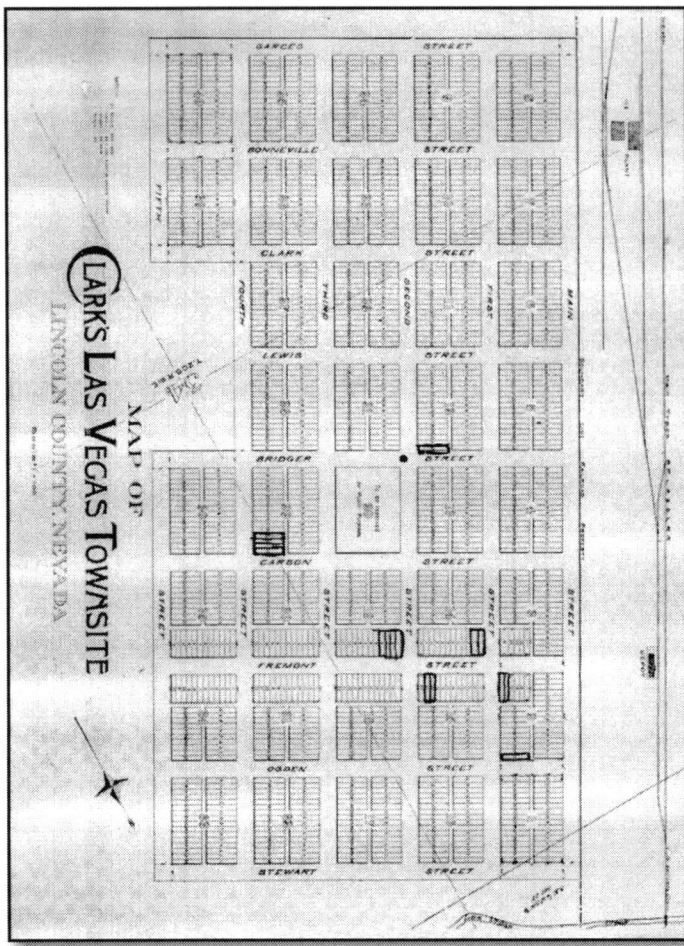

Lots purchased by W.R. Thomas are highlighted

4th street (south of the southwest corner with Carson Street) and one at the southwest corner of Bridger and 2nd. Over the next two months as the new town took off almost 150 temporary homes and businesses (tents and basic wooden structures) popped up, mostly on the business streets of Fremont and Main.

The directors of the First State Bank began building in October of 1905 a nice cement block building at the northeast corner of Fremont and 1st to replace their two-story wooden structure. William owned the two corner lots across from the bank on the northwest corner of Fremont and 1st and decided to build at that location the first two story block building in Las Vegas. He wanted it to house a nice large pharmacy along with storefronts on the lower floor and 16 rooms for offices and storage on the second floor. Planning began in August and construction began before the end of the year. The bank opened first in January of 1906 and the "Thomas Block" (as it was referred to in the local newspaper; street address numbers were not to be implemented until 1926 so many stores advertised by the name of the builder whose building they were in) was completed in May of 1906. After working on finishing touches, William was successful in leasing the pharmacy space (facing Fremont) to the Wilson Drug Co. in November.

Photo circa 1911 of the Thomas Block building at the northwest corner of Fremont and 1st Street
UNLV Libraries, Special Collections

A photo circa 1930 that shows the pharmacy building on the northwest corner of Fremont and 1st with the First State Bank on the northeast corner.
UNLV Libraries, Special Collections

Thomas was able to start a law practice in August 1905. His services covered corporate, mining and business law. He also handled divorces.

That same year he was chosen as one of the first local judges in Las Vegas. William became a charter member of the Masonic Lodge #32 (and would go on to serve one year from 1910 to 1911 as its Worshipful Master). In November of 1905 William became President of the Vegas Artesian Water Syndicate. In a matter of just 6 months, he had taken on the roles of builder, lawyer, and judge in addition to playing a big part in securing water for the new town.

Attorney ad in the September 12, 1908
Las Vegas Age newspaper

In early December of 1905 William became a grandfather. His older son Ralph and his wife had an 8-lb. baby girl, one of the first children born in Las Vegas.

Many of the people who purchased lots in the railroad's May 1905 auction were speculators who continued to live in Los Angeles. The water syndicate knew it would be expensive to drill artesian wells to supply the residents and businesses with sufficient water while waiting for the railroad to provide water. It was felt that all property owners should share in the cost. William was sent to Los Angeles to talk to the lot owners there to see if they would cooperate and pay their fair share. Not having built anything on their land, they refused to chip in. The syndicate decided to drill wells regardless, even though outside owners would stand to benefit from them. The first wells were sunk in early 1907 at a cost of some $5000.

Photo circa 1910 of the Thomas' family home at 4th and Carson
UNLV Libraries, Special Collections

In October of 1906 William made a run for the State Assembly. He won the local race in his Republican party but lost the final race to a Democrat. About a year later, William and Mary began construction of a nice home on their lots at Carson and 4th. It was bungalow style with brick walls and cobblestone pillars.

In late 1907 Thomas was chosen to serve on the town's advisory board and would travel to Pioche (the location of the Lincoln County seat) to represent the young town.

In May of 1908 William used two of his Fremont lots between 2nd and 3rd Streets to build basic cottages to rent out. Others would follow. In June he was chosen to go as a delegate to Reno to represent his Masonic Lodge. That summer there was a growing desire by residents of Las Vegas to have their area spin off from Lincoln County. Pioche was a long way from town and traveling there was not easy. In the summer of 1908, William volunteered to become a member of the "Division Club", a group of local businessmen who would start planning the logistics of how to break away from Lincoln County.

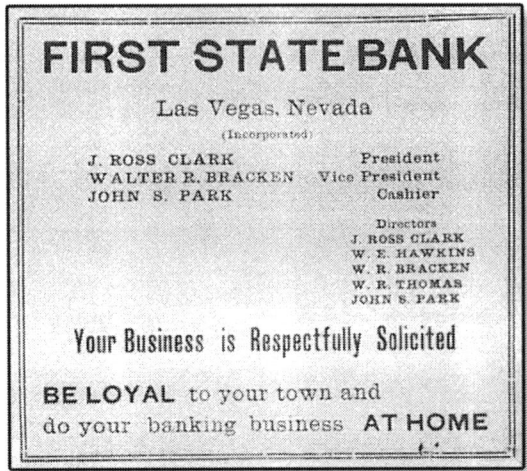

January 2, 1909, Las Vegas Age ad listing W.R. Thomas as one of its directors

In December of 1908 William served as a Republican to cast a Nevadan vote in the presidential electoral college. On January 1, 1909, he acquired a large amount of First State Bank stock and was chosen as one of its directors.

In early July of 1909, Lincoln County was split in two. The southern portion became Clark County. William Thomas was appointed the County's first District Attorney. His salary was $1500 per year. He traveled to Pioche a few weeks later to finalize the details of the separation. To publicize the new county to the outside world, a "Promotion Society" was created with William as its president. Some 5000 brochures were printed by the local town newspaper; they were distributed to businesses in Southern California and also placed in railroad depots throughout the Southwest U.S.

In September of 1909, a committee was organized to study a town sewer system. William acted as its chairman. The next month he was chosen to serve on the local school board and was in charge of teacher exams. In November he decided to sell his 80 undeveloped acres near the Old Ranch that he had purchased in early 1905. The buyer was a wealthy Arizona judge by the name of Kenneth Jackson who wanted to use the land for farming and ranching along with a winter home. He snapped up other properties in and out of town. Judge Jackson also bought William's shares in the Artesian Water Syndicate; William then resigned as its vice-president and gave up his seat on its board of directors.

William had allowed small businesses to build structures on his two lots on the southeast corner of Fremont and 1st. They were directly across Fremont from the bank and kitty-corner to his Thomas Block pharmacy building. Between 1905 and 1910, the corner housed a number of small temporary restaurants, a small drug store, a mercantile company and a grocery store. William had purchased the two prime lots at the railroad's auction for a hefty $2500. By early 1910 he was pulling in about $1000 a year in rent and his two lots were now valued at $10,000. He began ordering all his tenants to move off the two lots as he was planning to build a new permanent structure there. At the same time, he began plans to extend his pharmacy building further down North 1st Street for a meat market. Walls went up in June of 1910 and Tony Schweib's Meat Market opened in August.

A 1914 Mesquite Club photo. Mrs. Thomas is seen in front left center holding a hand fan. Daughter Marie is on far right with her left arm on the cement wall.
Courtesy of the Nevada State Museum, Las Vegas

William continued to serve as a school board trustee. He was master of ceremonies on July 2, 1910, for a cornerstone celebration at a new city school under construction. The next day he along with his wife Mary and daughter Marie rushed to Los Angeles. Son Ralph with his wife and young daughter Mary Louise were living in Los Angeles and all were very ill with diphtheria.

When they recovered William returned to Las Vegas. A few weeks later, Daughter Marie married Howard Espeset and they moved to Iowa. Howard was a cashier in his grandfather's bank. Marie was well educated having attended the Oberlin Conservatory of Music and schools in Florence, Italy.

In mid-July of 1910 William sold his "Thomas Block" to W.B. Wilson who had been leasing the pharmacy. William then focused his full attention to the new building he was preparing at the southeast corner of Fremont and 1st. All the structures were removed and excavation for a cellar was begun. In late August construction was underway on a two-story building that would be of concrete smooth-faced blocks.

Early undated photo of the completed two-story Mesquite Building on the southeast corner of Fremont and 1st Street
UNLV Libraries, Special Collections

In mid-August William declared his candidacy, this time as a Democrat, to run for judge of the Fourth District in Nevada. The nearest district court was extremely far away in Elko. Las Vegans really wanted and needed a local District Judge and court. William Thomas won his race in September and became the Judge of the 4th District, which raised his local status even further.

Younger son James was completing his education at Stanford University in California and was off in October 1910 to do further studies at Yale.

Work had stalled on Thomas' new building at the southeast corner of Fremont and 1st. Construction resumed on first floor work on October 22, 1910. By mid-February of 1911 the building was completed. The structure was named the "Mesquite Building" and officially opened on April 15, 1911.

William opened law offices on the second floor which also had large spaces with lots of windows. The young Las Vegas-Tonopah Railroad rented some office space on the second floor as did local lodges. Downstairs was split between a small mercantile store operated by W.E. Hawkins and a large grocery store on the corner with large plate glass windows operated by Ralph Thomas (no relation to William). The grocery store became the first one in town to give exact change in pennies and all sales had to be in cash. It had nice rugs, fine fixtures, wicker rockers, a writing desk with free stationery and phone service. It also had adjustable shelves, ceiling lights with brass chains, two 12-foot-long counters, six display cases and modern Toledo weight scales.

WE ARE

Certainly Doing THE *Grocery Business! Watch Our Windows for More* BARGAINS

MESQUITE GROCERY CO.,
'PHONE
ONE15FIVE

May 6, 1911 Las Vegas Age newspaper ad for the Mesquite Grocery Co.

Las Vegas became a city in 1911 and Judge Thomas helped frame the city charter. When the city's Chamber of Commerce formed in 1911, William served on its Auditing and Finance Committee and would become a long-term member. That summer Judge Thomas took a well deserved one month trip back to South Dakota to visit old friends.

In 1912, William became the president of the Las Vegas Home Builders Corporation. That September he ran for the Nevada State Supreme Court as a Progressive Party candidate. The party was created by Teddy Roosevelt. William campaigned throughout Nevada. In late October he travelled up north and was well received by a large crowd at the Carson Opera House. There were four candidates in the race. Judge Thomas came in a close second to Pat McCarran in Clark County. State-wide voting resulted in him coming in second with 303 votes; the winner had 334 votes.

During the first week of January 1913 William's new Mesquite Building experienced a flooded basement due to a high water table in the area. Remediation was very expensive. A new water system at a depth of ten feet went under the adjacent roads which helped solve the problem.

In early 1913 William Thomas made a bold prediction -- that someday Las Vegas would be home to some 400,000 people. At the time, its population was under 2,000. The city had a large July 4th celebration and William was a key speaker, presenting for some five minutes. The month prior, William took on a law practice partner by the name of A.S. Henderson. Henderson was also serving as the town's school principal. When he was appointed City Attorney the following year, he resigned from the law practice. He would go on to be Clark County District Attorney.

Tragedy struck the Williams family in September of 1913. Mary had been in poor health for several years and was living with son Ralph and his family in Los Angeles. She passed away on September 25 and was buried in Los Angeles.

A few weeks later William announced plans to build his third large building in town; this one was to be a hotel on his northeast corner lots near Fremont and 2nd. Construction began in April of 1914, but complications brought the project to a standstill. (He eventually sold the lots and later on the Apache Hotel was built on the lots.) Two months earlier, now having completed his education, younger son James married and moved into the family home at 4th and Carson.

In October of 1914 William partnered with Dr. Roy Martin to purchase the large "Sund Section" of land just outside of town (now the Chinatown area of Las Vegas) for $10,000. It already had a well. Judge Thomas and Dr. Martin would sell the land for a nice profit to L. Lindsey of Los Angeles in 1916.

William was chosen as vice-president of the Chamber of Commerce in December 1914. Two weeks later, on December 18, son James and his wife had a child named William Raymond Thomas after his grandfather. Sadly, the baby died shortly thereafter on January 1, 1915.

In May of 1915 William made another trip to South Dakota. After returning he went to Los Angeles to spend some time with son Ralph and his family. He longed for his Las Vegas which he referred to as "God's Country". He returned on August 14 in a new Dodge automobile.

In the summer of 1916, son James, now living in Southern California became the editor of the Santa Monica Daily Sun newspaper. In November of 1917 William went on a long car trip with three friends to Tonopah. Their drive home was a rough one. It took some 15 hours and William announced the "roads were none too good".

In May of 1918 William laid the cement foundation for a new garage on the south side of Fremont, fifty feet east of 2nd Street. In June he filed to run to seek the judgeship for the 10th Judicial District which covered Clark and Lincoln Counties. He lost in September, coming in last in a three-man race.

William's health began to decline in 1919. In late 1918 he had come down with the Spanish influenza which took its toll on him. Many also believed he remained depressed after losing his wife in 1913. He sold his law practice and law library in September of 1919 to A.W. Ham and announced his plans to move to Hollywood, California to live in retirement with his daughter Marie who was now residing there.

In early January of 1920 he experienced eight days of bad indigestion. Good friend Dr. Roy Martin came from Las Vegas to tend to him. Specialists were summoned to examine William but agreed that there was no hope for a recovery. William R. Thomas passed away at 10:25 p.m. on January 21, 1920, at the age of 64 due to heart failure. He was buried in the Hollywood Cemetery. The District Court in Las Vegas adjourned in his memory when it learned of his death.

Son Ralph handled his estate valued at over $110,000. His properties, possessions, and some stocks were left to his three children -- Ralph, James and Marie. The pharmacy building was razed in 1955. The Mesquite Building was eventually knocked down and the corner land became part of the Golden Nugget Casino. In 1920 son Ralph was appointed to fill a vacant seat on the Las Vegas city commission. Son James would leave Southern California and move to Berkeley, California and then San Francisco.

William R. Thomas was a very distinguished Las Vegas citizen who served his community faithfully for almost 15 years. His buildings may now be gone, but his vast contributions to the early growth and development of Las Vegas should never be forgotten.

Chapter 5
John and Adam Kramer
Barbers

As the town of Las Vegas got its start in the first half of 1905, people from many faraway places were taking a chance on a new life in a hot, dusty, and fairly uninviting desert environment. They were perhaps foolishly leaving their homes in safe and established distant communities to seek adventure and fortune in the middle of nowhere.

The railroad brought the desert town of Las Vegas to life. With the coming of the tracks to the area, folks knew this roughly midway point on the journey between Southern California and Salt Lake City might be an important growth hub as it had sufficient water to support life and businesses along with needs of the railroad.

There was an immediate need for supplies and services. A bank was formed, lawyers appeared out of thin air, and the railroad planned to provide needed general services and utilities. Naturally, the first merchants offered goods such as food, clothes, household staples, heating oil and building materials. Doctors and dentists soon set up practices and simple tent hotels offered beds. Being a town of mostly men, there was definitely a need for barbers. Barbershops not only offered haircuts and shaves, they were also a place to bathe. Before the end of 1905 there were already three barbershops in the railroad's town. Researching the early barbers of Las Vegas, one quickly learns how frequently they changed locations. Some had their own basic barbershops while others rented out a chair here or there until they had enough funds to invest in their own operation.

The Adam Kramer family in a 1920 photo
Courtesy of Martha Kramer Bryant, granddaughter of Adam Kramer

The first barbers to arrive were brothers John (born in 1871) and Adam (born in 1875) Kramer who came from Pennsylvania. Their parents were Christian and Leah Kramer who had five children. Father Christian was a tobacconist. Adam worked for the local railroad and had also served in the Navy during the Spanish-American War. He had seen duty in Cuba, China, and the Philippines. In September of 1903 John, a barber in Bedford, Pennsylvania had relocated to Los Angeles. The brothers came to Las Vegas a month or so prior to the railroad's land auction with John arriving first.

John David Kramer had married Anna Mary Price on December 24, 1894. He was 23 and she was 25. All four of their children were born in nearby Maryland -- Martha Jane (1895), John Jr. (1897), David (1899), and Sherman (1903).

Brother Adam Henry Kramer married Laura Belle Definbaugh on April 17, 1905, in Cumberland, Maryland just before leaving for Las Vegas. He was 29 and she was 26. They would have six children after arriving in their new home -- a baby boy in 1906 who died a few days after birth from excessive heat, Clifford (1907), Edna (1909), Doris (1911), Frances (1914), and Mary "Jane" (1916).

Upon arriving in Las Vegas, John secured a job barbering in John Wisner's small establishment in McWilliams' township. Adam established his own barbershop nearby, across from the bank on Wilson Avenue. It was constructed of canvas and wood siding. The brothers eagerly attended the railroad's land auction On May 15, 1905. Adam purchased Lots 6 and 7 of Block 14, which was on the south side of Fremont midway between 1st and 2nd Streets. The brothers erected a 12 by 18 foot temporary tent there and became the first ones to occupy a structure along the empty block.

1906 photo of young Fremont Street looking west. Adam Kramer purchased two lots on the fairly empty street on the left.
UNLV Libraries, Special Collections

Like so many others, the Kramer families had exited McWilliams' less favored townsite.

The brothers set up a barbershop on their other lot next to their tent in the summer of 1905 but soon moved to a new location around the corner on South 1st Street.

A rare photo of south Fremont St., between 1st and 2nd. Circa 1908.
A barbershop and pole, possibly that of the Kramer's earlier store,
can been seen just to the left of center.
Courtesy of the Nevada State Museum, Las Vegas

Robert Lake is the older man on the right
UNLV Libraries, Special Collections

They took on a partner by the name of Robert Lake, Sr. Their shop had large mirrors and a linoleum floor. Robert Lake opened his own barbershop further north on 1st Street in the Arcade Saloon.

In November of 1905 Lake moved his operation into larger quarters that could accommodate more chairs. He settled in the Turf Saloon on North 1st St. in Block 16 (which was set aside by the railroad for liquor sales, gambling, and inevitably brothels).

When Judge William Thomas completed building his impressive cement "Thomas Block" two-story structure on the northwest corner of Fremont and 1st, a large pharmacy opened and the Kramer's secured a lease for a spot adjacent to it.

The Arcade Saloon is the taller structure on the right
UNLV Libraries, Special Collections

They moved in by April of 1906 and began advertising frequently in the local Las Vegas Age newspaper. In June, Lake put his barber shop in the Turf Saloon up for sale. It took some six months for him to find a buyer.

In late 1906 John Kramer decided he wanted to move his family to Greenwater, a mining community in Nye County, where he would open a saloon. He sold his interest in the barber shop to a Mr. Schniedman. Schniedman didn't last long, selling his half interest to Robert Lake in early 1907. Lake and Adam Kramer became partners once again, calling their business the "Gold Nugget Barber Shop". Lake advertised "amputations without pain" and placed an order for two new porcelain bathtubs. Another partner joined them in April of 1907, a Mr. Kerner. Baths were advertised at four for a dollar and haircuts were 35-cents. A shower was installed. A May 1907 newspaper ad for the barbershop had a Mr. Paladeaux listed as a proprietor. In August Louis Wulle from Salt Lake City rented a chair at the shop.

The Kramer's barbershop was on the corner just to the right of the pharmacy entrance. If you look carefully, you can see their barber pole just to the right of the corner.
Courtesy of the Nevada State Museum, Las Vegas.

In late September 1907 Adam Kramer begin work on building his own barbershop on Fremont Street, between Main and 1st on a lot he had just purchased. It was of adobe bricks and cost him $1200. While it was being built, another barber joined the Gold Nugget, one Mr. Dofflelmyre. Adam's structure was done in late November 1907. He had three barber

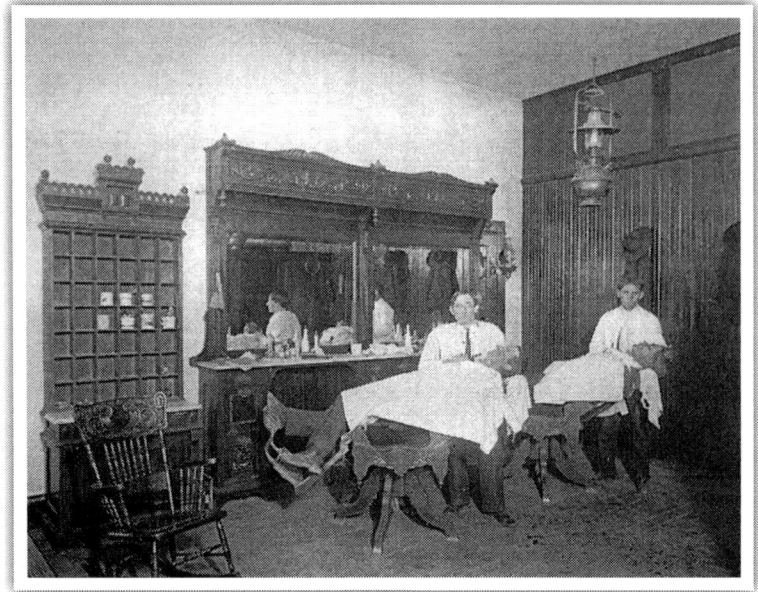

A photo circa 1910 showing the interior of a typical Las Vegas barbershop
UNLV Libraries, Special Collections

chairs and opened in December. He continued to be a partner in the Gold Nugget Barber Shop with Robert Lake and others. In early 1908 they began operating a laundry business in their barber shop with suits and pants cleaned and pressed ($2 for suits and 75-cents for pants).

Things apparently didn't work out as expected in Greenwater for brother John. He returned to Las Vegas and in June of 1908 bought out Lake's interest in the Gold Nugget. He was now partners with his brother once again. John quickly installed a large electric fan to help keep the store cooler over the summer. He also built a home further east on Fremont Street and in December his wife Anna purchased a "Mehling" piano for the home.

In April of 1909 Adam Kramer opened the "Palace Barber Shop" on Fremont. It was in a row of ground floor shop fronts that were part of the Hotel Nevada expansion near Main Street. He was next to Will Beckley's clothing store. Adam advertised shaves for 15-cents, haircuts for 35-cents, and baths for 35-cents. He also hawked "Kramer's Desert Holly Mixture", a cure for dandruff and eczema. That was followed in October by an olive oil shampoo that would "cure dandruff as well as reducing falling out hair".

In late December of 1909, all the town's competing barbers came to an agreement to close weekdays at 7 p.m. and at 10 p.m. on Saturdays. On Sundays and holidays, they would close at noon. Three barbershops were now operating, according to the local newspaper.

In the summer of 1910, Adam got into a physical confrontation with the town's tough but popular sheriff, Sam Gay. Not smart. He was fined one dollar for his mistake.

Like other well-to-do families in the young town, the Kramer wives and children would find cooler locales to spend their summers. Over the years, they took many vacations to California or made visits to family back in Pennsylvania.

In early 1911 the Isis Theater on the south side of Fremont, just west of Thomas' Department Store, was razed to make way for the new twenty room 2-story Las Vegas Hotel being built by Beale and Horden. Downstairs along Fremont there were to be three new shops. The Kramer brothers leased one of the spaces.

Photo of the Las Vegas Hotel in the July 27, 1912, Las Vegas Age. The window of the shop on the left says, "J. D. Kramer Baths".

Adam then sold his interest in Lots 6 and 7 of Block 14 for $4000. John moved out of the Gold Nugget to operate in the new location. It opened in late May 1911. Adam kept his Hotel Nevada shop but was a partner with brother John in the Las Vegas Hotel shop. John installed a 192 gallon water tank for hot baths in the new shop. In July the town instituted many new types of required business licenses. The Kramer's each paid $7.50 for their one-year barber licenses.

Another view of the south side of Fremont between Main and 1st. circa 1915. Beckley's clothing store was on the left of the barbershop and Las Vegas Hotel.
Courtesy of the Nevada State Museum, Las Vegas

Adam had a family home on 1st Street. In October of 1911 he had it moved to No. 3rd Street near Ogden. On the old lot he put in a foundation for a new one-story barbershop. It would be composed of metal lath and cement plaster. In January of 1912 Adam sold his half interest in the Las Vegas Hotel barber shop. W.E. Arnold and A.D. Lisonbee became John Kramer's new partners. A Mr. Adams soon replaced Lisonbee. There was a big fire in the adjacent Thomas' Department Store in May of 1912. John's barber shop experienced $150 in water damage.

John sold his interest in the barbershop to his employee George Sanderson in July of 1912. He used his gained funds to buy an interest with Walter Houck in the Colorado Hotel. In October of 1912 Adam returned to the Las Vegas Hotel barber shop, buying a 50% interest from Mr. Arnold.

Clark County was formed in 1909 when the area broke away from Lincoln County and Las Vegas became a city in 1911. The Kramer brothers began to show an increased interest in local affairs in 1912 and 1913. John was elected Clark County Public Administrator in November of 1912 and probably barbered no more. He handled the settling of estates and received a $5,000 per year salary. Adam became head of the local Socialist party and in April of 1913 made an unsuccessful run for a seat on the Clark County Commission.

In early 1913 Adam's new building on 1st Street was completed. He opened a barbershop that operated there at least into 1915. He had leased his barbershop on Fremont in May of 1914 to Joe Flores and Otto Winterhalter who opened a pool hall, cigar stand, and a barbershop of their own. They called it "The Southern" as it was next to the Northern Club on its west.

It is not known exactly when Adam retired from the barbering business. It is possible that sometime in 1914 that John and Anna divorced as John is reported to be living in Idaho in 1915 and moving to San Francisco. His wife Anna continued to live in Las Vegas and managed family affairs and interests.

In May of 1922 John visited Las Vegas. In November of 1923 Anna sold her home and moved to Long Beach, California to live with one of her sons. John was listed in the 1930 Census as living in Chula Vista, California by himself and ranching.

Adam and wife Laura remained in Las Vegas. After being in poor health for some time, Adam suffered a major heart attack and died on January 30, 1938. He left an estate estimated at $10,000 and was buried in Woodlawn Cemetery. He was 62 years old. Laura continued to reside at 802 So. 2nd Street and by 1949 was living at 714 So. 6th Street.

She still owned numerous properties in town. At some point she moved to Hawaii to live with daughter Doris. Laura passed away in 1968 at age 90 and was buried alongside husband Adam in Woodlawn.

1923 photo of the home Adam and Laura built on South 2nd St
Courtesy of Nancy Kramer Bryant

Circa 1937 photo of Adam and Laura Kramer
Courtesy of Nancy Kramer Bryant

The gravesite marker at Woodlawn Cemetery for Laura and Adam Kramer
Find a Grave Website

John's wife Anna lived out her life in Long Beach and passed away in 1964. She was about 95 years old. John lived to the ripe old age of 101, passing away on May 14, 1972 in San Diego. No photo that could be positively confirmed to be that of John Kramer could be located.

Anna Kramer at age 52 is on the left in this May of 1947 photo
UNLV Libraries, Special Collections; Charles Aplin Photo Collection(0236 0036)

Grave marker of John Kramer
Find A Grave Website

As mentioned earlier, John and Anna had four children. Their oldest, Martha, married twice and went on to live in Los Angeles where she would pass away. She had one child.

Their second child, John Jr., was a railroad blacksmith in the 1920's. He would move to the San Diego area, marry and have two children. He died in 1983.

John and Anna's third child, David, served in WWI aboard the U.S.S Rainbow and was discharged in February of 1919 due to a damaged eardrum (the result of cannon fire). He was a Las Vegas fireman after the war and married Daisy French in July of 1920. Their son Jack, born in 1922, became a famous tennis celebrity who won many prestigious tournaments.

Martha is the second from the left in this school photo circa 1913
UNLV Libraries, Special Collections

David passed away in 1983.

Their fourth and youngest child, son Sherman, was a railroad blacksmith in the 1920's. He married Thelma Olsen in 1926. In the 1930 U.S. Census, he was listed as a roomer in Ruth, Nevada which was a mining town just to the northwest of Ely, Nevada. He was a welder for the copper mines. In the 1940 Census he was listed as being in construction, living in Boulder City with second wife Helen. Sherman passed away in the Los Angeles area in 1970 at age 66.

Tennis player Jack Kramer, approaching retirement, is on the left receiving a trophy in this 1947 Las Vegas Age newspaper photo

And what became of Adam and Laura's five children? Their first born, Clifford, was involved with the Hoover Dam project as a machinist. In 1933 he married Ada Rockefeller in St. George, Utah. In 1936 they had daughter Nancy who I was able to locate. She lives in Mesquite, NV and was most helpful in sharing family history and photographs with me. In the early 1940's Clifford worked for the U.S. Bureau of Reclamation. He went on to serve in World War II. He later returned to work at the dam. Clifford retired in 1960 and passed away in 1983 at age 75. He was buried in a Beaver, Utah cemetery.

Sister Edna in April of 1927 was one of only 15 graduates of Las Vegas High School. She would marry and become Mrs. Edna Kramer Wadsworth. She passed away young in 1946 at about age 37 and was buried in Woodlawn Cemetery.

Sister Doris married Reid Lumsden of Texas who became a distinguished pilot in WWII. Major Lumsden passed in 1994 at age 83 and Doris in 2003 at age 91. They were buried in Honolulu.

Las Vegas High School photo of Doris Kramer taken in 1929
UNLV Libraries, Special Collections; Las Vegas High School Class of 1929 Photo Collection (0109 0002)

Sister Frances attended the University of Nevada in Reno. She married Wheeler Doll in 1938 in Santa Barbara, California. They went on to live in Glendale, California where Frances died in 1963 at age 49.

Final sibling Mary "Jane" married Virgil S. Haugse in 1939 in Boulder City, Nevada. She passed in 2014 at about age 88.

In November of 1968 after mother Laura Kramer passed away, her children held a family reunion. It was the first time they were together in some 22 years. All surviving children of Anna and Laura attended.

So why write about barbers who bounced around from one location to another? John and Adam were early pioneer merchants who saw to the needs of other early pioneers. They offered shaves, haircuts and baths to satisfy the hygiene needs of the local population. They were just as important as other merchants. They made life more tolerable and pleasant for the people that settled and built early Las Vegas. They deserve proper recognition.

Chapter 6
The Boggs Brothers
Tobacco, Confectionary, and Ice Cream Merchants

In early Las Vegas if you wanted a cigar, some sweets, or a refreshing fountain drink on a hot day you knew who the Boggs brothers were. For some 25 years they dealt in tobacco products, refreshments, confectionaries, and groceries. They operated businesses that met many a need of the town's early residents.

Benjamin Franklin Boggs and his brother Orren Clinton Boggs were born in Ohio in the 1870's. Their parents were Benjamin Franklin Boggs, Sr. (1846 - 1928) and Lydia Kniesley Boggs (1846 - 1882). They were married in 1866 and had seven children, all born in an Ohio log cabin about 50 miles outside of Cincinnati -- Corasell ("Cora") in 1867, Charles in 1868, William ("Sherman") in 1870, Ben Franklin Jr. in 1872, Arba ("John") in 1874, Orren in 1876, and finally Ellsworth in 1880. The Boggs raised their kids on a farm about 40 miles south of Toledo. Sometime before mother Lydia's death in 1882 (at age 36) the family relocated for a short time to Columbia, Kansas before moving on to Denver, Colorado where Frank Sr. was a contractor.

Benjamin Franklin Boggs liked to be called Frank and his brother Orren went by his middle name Clint. In Denver, older brother Frank would find work for the Denver Power Company and also toiled in a furniture house. He remained in Denver until 1894 when he went to Cripple Creek, Colorado to do mining. From there he went for about a decade to the mines in the Rhyolite and Bullfrog regions of Nevada. Meanwhile, brother Clint spent his youth in Denver and in his late 20's relocated to Southern Nevada to try his hand at agriculture and mining.

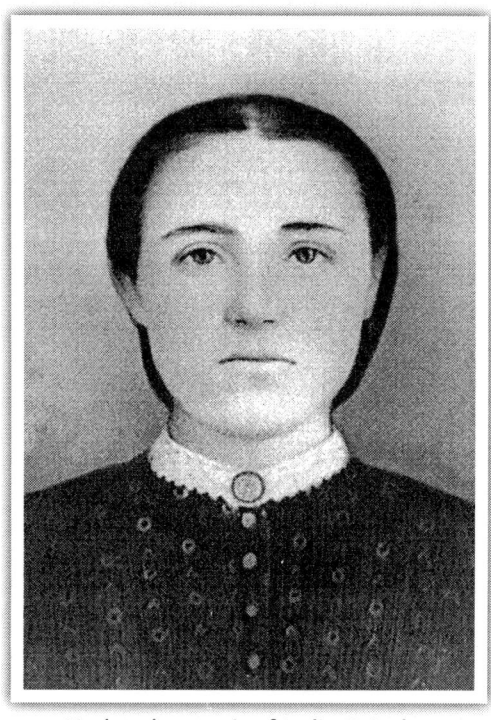
Undated portrait of Lydia Kniesley

Frank arrived in Las Vegas first showing up as a guest in Ladd's tent hotel on April 23, 1905. Even though he was in Las Vegas at the time, it is not known if Frank purchased any lots in the railroad's May land auction. He did do some successful prospecting on and off for about a year at a mine in the Vincent District.

October 7, 1905, Las Vegas Times ad for Boggs & Co. operated by B.F. Boggs and O.D. Hicks

Frank partnered with a 30 year old gold miner living in town by the name of Orin DeTar Hicks who went by O.D. Hicks. They opened a small temporary candy and ice cream store somewhere on 1st Street.

By late 1905 the beautiful First State Bank building was being completed at the northeast corner of Fremont and 1st Streets. On the east side of 1st Street directly north of the bank, a few simple storefronts had already been built. Each wanting their own business, Frank rented one of the spaces and O.D. Hicks rented an adjacent one.

Page 37

Boggs & Co. was located just to the north of the Shady Cafe in this undated photo
UNLV Libraries, Special Collections

They decided to partner in their ventures and connected them by tearing out the wall between them. Equipment and fixtures were ordered for "Boggs & Co.". They sold ice cream, tobacco products, candy, and 5-cent sodas. As their business took off through 1906, they added a power freezer and ice crushing machine at the rear of their shop to begin wholesale manufacturing of ice cream which they were able to sell in Rhyolite.

In February of 1907 brother Clint arrived for the first time in Las Vegas. He had been in charge of the Lucky Strike Mine which had a rich vein of ore. O.D. Hicks wanted to move to Tampa, Florida to join his brother in a brokerage. Clint stepped in and bought out his share of the business which was then renamed "Boggs Bros.". The brothers got creative that cold winter when soda and ice cream sales slowed and brought in a pool table and also began selling coal for $15 a ton. They refreshed their shop with new wallpaper.

In early 1908 they left their store on North 1st Street for nicer quarters in a new building next to the Las Vegas Pharmacy on the north side of Fremont, just west of 1st Street.

They opened up in March after purchasing the lot from Perry L. Smith and their old location on 1st was leased by the Telephone Exchange. Their father Frank Sr. visited in April of 1908 and decided to move to Las Vegas from Denver. He would help his sons in their store as they continued to grow their wholesale ice cream business.

Some remodeling was done in 1909 and in the summer of 1910, they purchased the grocery stock of Adolph Levy; thus adding general food products to their inventory.

Boggs Bros. Groceries is seen to the left of the Las Vegas Pharmacy in this undated photo
UNLV Libraries, Special Collections

When the Las Vegas Hotel opened in 1912 directly across the street on Fremont, the brothers decided to rent space on the ground floor for their tobacco and confectionary business. They continued to sell groceries on the north side of the street adjacent to the pharmacy for a few months before they sold their business to M.C. Thomas who was looking for a temporary store to run his grocery operation out of after suffering a devastating fire in his large store at the southwest corner of Fremont and 1st Streets.

O.D. Hicks and his wife Maude (age 27) who went to Florida in 1907 were only away for a few years. They returned in March of 1911 and in the summer of 1912 O.D. joined the Boggs brothers in their hotel confectionary and tobacco store.

In October of 1912 Frank moved into a new concrete home at 5th and Ogden. During the summer of 1913 the Boggs' went on a long three month driving trip to the west coast in a new Cadillac. The brothers visited San Francisco, Sacramento, Oregon, Truckee, Reno and Goldfield.

Changes were coming to the business. O.D. and Maude Hicks in late 1913 decided to move again, this time to Oregon. A few months later, Frank wanted to try ranching in Northern California (Modoc County in the far northeast portion of the state) which he did for some ten years. With O.D. and Frank gone, Clint was now the sole proprietor of the hotel confectionary and tobacco store. Clint resided by himself on South 9th Street.

In April of 1916 the "City Bakery" took over the Boggs Bros. location on the north side of Fremont Street.

In March of 1917 Clint purchased a new Ford. In September of 1919 he was caught speeding and paid a $40 fine after spending a night in jail.

Things did not work out in Oregon for O.D. Hicks and he had returned to Las Vegas where in 1916 he served a short term as a city commissioner of finance. He passed in 1918 at age 43 and was buried in an unmarked grave in Woodlawn Cemetery. In April of 1920 Clint married O.D.'s widow Maude who was about 40 years of age.

After marrying they drove to visit Frank on his California ranch. They had no children.

Circa 1920's photo of Maude Hicks-Boggs in the upper left
Courtesy of the Nevada State Museum, Las Vegas

Brother Frank also married in 1920. On July 3, 1920, Frank married Lura Jeanette Owens on his ranch in northeastern California.

Lura and Frank Boggs in an undated photo
Ancestry.org

She was about 29 years old. They would have four children -- Barbara (1921), Lois "Edna" Boggs Sargent (1922), Mabel (1926) and Frank (1927).

Clint's wife Maude passed away in June of 1925 from tuberculosis. She was buried at Woodlawn and among her pallbearers were distinguished residents Walter Bracken, Jake and Will Beckley, and William Ferron. Clint would wed again in June of 1929 in St. George, Utah. His new bride was Jane Fayle Jean Henderson Boggs (age 46).

Undated early photo of Jean Fayle Boggs

Jane's first husband had been George Arthur Fayle, one of the prominent founders of Goodsprings, Nevada. He died during the 1918 influenza. Jane was born in Glasgow, Scotland and came to the United States at age 10. She had a daughter (Jean Nevada Fayle Purdue) with George Fayle in 1910.

Undated photo of B.F. Boggs, Sr.
Ancestry.org

Clint Boggs in a 1930 Rotary Club photo
*UNLV Libraries, Special Collections;
Scoop Garside Photo Collection (0067 0016)*

In 1928 father Franklin Boggs Sr. passed away and was buried in an unmarked grave in Woodlawn Cemetery. He was close to 83 years old.

Clint was elected city treasurer in April of 1929.

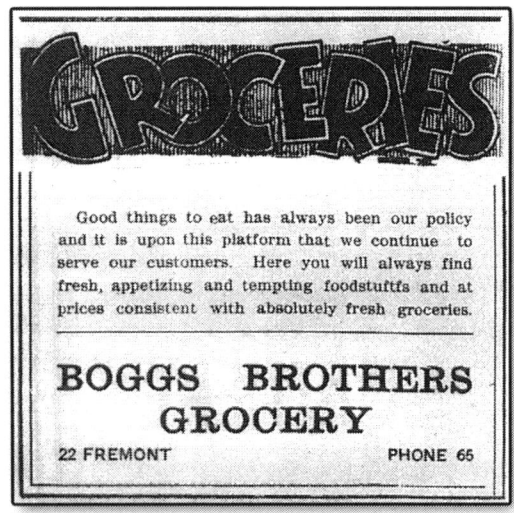

February 21, 1928, Las Vegas Age ad

March 27, 1928, Las Vegas Age ad

By this time, Frank and his wife left their California ranch and had returned to live in Las Vegas. Frank had rejoined Clint in business. The brothers continued to sell tobacco, ice cream, groceries, and candy through 1930.

They had constructed a large two story building at 319 Fremont St. and J. C. Penney decided to move their store from next to the Overland Hotel on Fremont east of Main into their new large building. The second floor of the structure was done in a Spanish style and had a balcony and tiled roof. It offered modern heating and cooling. Frank and Clint sold their building in 1931 and retired. Frank was content looking after his mining interests.

August 30, 1930, Las Vegas Age ad for Clint's campaign for Sheriff

In 1930 Clint ran to become Sheriff but lost to Joe Keate.

In October 1932 he was appointed by the city commissioners to be the Chief of Police. In 1934 he ran to continue on as chief and was elected, serving until June of 1935. After his stint as chief, Clint went on to dabbling in real estate. He also enjoyed fishing and hunting trips.

In June of 1947 Clint was on a fishing trip on Lake Mead when he suffered a serious heart attack. He died at age 71 while on the way to the Clark County General Hospital.

Clint was buried in Woodlawn Cemetery.

His estate estimated at $50,000 along with investment income of some $5,000 per year went to his wife Jean. In January of 1950 Jean passed at age 66 from a heart attack and was buried in the Goodsprings Cemetery.

Frank Boggs would die on October 8, 1951, at age 79 and was buried in Woodlawn Cemetery. His second wife, Lura, passed away on July 3, 1985, at about age 94 and was buried beside him.

The Boggs brothers shall be remembered as distinguished Las Vegas merchants who spent many years in business in the early years of Las Vegas with Clint serving terms as city treasurer and chief of police.

Undated photo of Clint Boggs taken sometime just before his death in 1947
Ancestry.org

Woodlawn grave marker for Clint Boggs
Billion Graves website

Jean Fayle Boggs' headstone in the Goodsprings Cemetery
Find A Grave website

Undated photo of Laura Owens Boggs later in her life
Ancestry.org

Laura and Frank in a circa early 1940's photo
Ancestry.org

Grave marker in Woodlawn Cemetery for Frank and Laura Boggs
Billion Graves website

Chapter 7
Ivan Botkin
Clothing Merchant

Ivan Wilfred Botkin is certainly an unknown to most people. Ivan's full first name was Ivanhoe and in the early local papers he was referred to as I.W. Botkin. He was born on April 15, 1884, in Denver, Colorado. As a young man Ivan moved to Cheyenne, Wyoming where he was employed by the Union Pacific Railroad as a machinist. By the spring of 1905 he had made his way to Las Vegas. He established a small clothing store in McWilliams' Townsite and found lodging in a tent rooming house.

Ivan was just one of the many businessmen who quickly moved out of McWilliams' town to establish a store in the new more promising railroad town on the other side of the tracks. He found a partner by the name of Block to establish the new town's first all-clothing store on the north side of Fremont between 1st and 2nd Streets which was still virtually empty. They called their enterprise "Block & Botkin Gent's Furnishings" and began advertising in the local papers. Their store was unusual as it was actually two adjacent stores that had two show windows and two entrances. Their motto was "quick sales and small profits".

Mr. Block decided to sell his half of the store to Botkin in late October of 1905. Ivan added a "living room" in the back of his store for patrons to rest. His business was renamed "Ivan Botkin Clothing".

Summer of 1905 photo of Block & Botkin store. There is an excellent chance that the men posing in the photo are Block and Botkin. No photos of Botkin could be found. Notice the two doors and two windows in the photo.
Courtesy of the Nevada State Museum, Las Vegas

In December of 1905 at age 21, Ivan returned to Cheyenne, Wyoming to marry bookkeeper Bertha Taylor who he had met the year before leaving for Las Vegas. They returned to Nevada and lived in the rear of his shop. The population of Las Vegas was very small in 1905 and merchants often socialized with each other. They would take turns hosting dinners at their homes and would begin the formation of numerous social circles, clubs, and fraternities. The Botkin's along with five other couples formed the "Jolly Dozen Card Club" and they also participated in a whist club.

In September 1906 Ivan's two adjacent shops were merged into one with nice show windows. The entire store continued to sell men's furnishings. The beautiful and busy First State Bank was now operating in a new cement block building on the corner of 1st Street four doors to the west of Botkin's store and helped bring in customers.

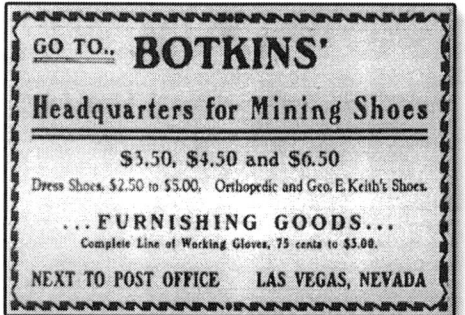

May 12, 1906, Las Vegas Times ad

GENTS' FURNISHING GOODS
Hamilton-Brown Shoes
I. W. BOTKIN
Fremont St., Las Vegas.

November 2, 1907, Las Vegas Age ad

A 1912 Mesquite Club photo showing Bertha Botkin
Courtesy of the Nevada State Museum, Las Vegas

In January of 1908 Ivan Botkin became secretary of a fraternity called the Las Vegas Aerie, #213, F. O. E. It met every Thursday evening in the Eagle's Hall. In May of 1908 Ivan volunteered to serve on a committee charged with organizing a volunteer fire department. Bertha became treasurer of the Ladies Guild.

In December, the Age newspaper talked of the beautiful neckwear, suspenders, hose, and Christmas items on display in Botkin's show windows. Suits were selling from $13 to $46. Business was good.

In 1909, Botkin knew it was time to move on from his wooden store and construct a sturdier permanent block building. In May he began soliciting bids. He rejected two initial bids for $9,500 and $13,700 as they both lacked paint, glass, and electrical components. In July he moved his store just to the east to clear his lot for his new brick building. He settled on an $8,000 bid and his new store would open in March of 1910. Now with more room, he was able to greatly expand his line of shoe offerings. Ivan brought in a young cousin as an employee.

In 1910, Ivan became an active member of the local gun club. The men would find areas outside of town to have competitions and results were often published in the town's newspaper. In late August of 1910 Ivan announced his candidacy as a Democrat running for the position of the county's recorder and auditor. He would lose in the November election. Just a few days later, his mother would die in a California automobile accident. Ivan would take time off work to travel to California and then escort her body to Denver for burial.

Botkin decided to move his operation further to the west on Fremont Street in February of 1911. He leased the spot adjacent to the large pharmacy at the northwest corner of Fremont and 1st Street that had been occupied by J.D. Kramer's Barber Shop. He signed a three-year lease. After moving over his stock, he was able to rent out spaces in his brick building near the bank. In March, he and Bertha purchased a cottage on 4th Street and began remodeling it. A new cement porch was installed along with a modern bathroom, an oak front door, and fancy windows from Iowa. In 1911, a mining company called Gold Legion Consolidated was formed with Ivan as its secretary. It took over seven mining claims in the Nob Hill region near Searchlight.

Doing well as a business owner, Ivan Botkin along with other successful merchants would begin financially backing surety bonds. When men were elected to office, the city required them to take out a surety bond to protect the city against any wrongdoing they may do. Merchants like Botkin would financially back those bonds for an annual fee from the office holder.

A new larger court house was being built in 1913 and until it was completed in 1914 Ivan was able to rent out space in his building east of the bank for temporary court usage.

With his three year lease up on the store next to the pharmacy and the new court house now open, in 1914 Ivan decided to return his business back to his building. That summer, Botkin would file to run for the city's Public Administrator and Bertha would make a trip back to Cheyenne, Wyoming to visit family. Ivan would lose his race in a close vote of 461 to 452. Bertha would take a bookkeeping job for the M.C. Thomas Department Store at the southwest corner of Fremont and 1st Street.

Most of the merchants in early Las Vegas obtained their stock from large companies in Los Angeles. It was easy to transport their merchandise by train to Las Vegas. There is a mysterious gap of one year from late 1914 to late 1915 about Botkin. In early October of 1915 we learn in the Las Vegas Age that Botkin's building and business on Fremont Street had been "attached" by the Los Angeles Board of Trade. One can only surmise that for some reason Botkin had failed to pay for purchases made in Los Angeles. Later that month, a sheriff's auction was held, and a Los Angeles bidder bought Ivan's store fixtures for $1050. In November of 1916 Bertha and Ivan divorced. (They never had any children.) W.I. Roberts was able to buy Botkin's building in early 1917 and opened his undertaking company in the rear of the structure. Botkin had probably left Las Vegas sometime in 1917.

After her divorce from Ivan, Bertha began using her maiden name of Taylor. About five months later she would marry Howard Turner. Ivan's WWI draft registration card indicates he was residing in Tonopah, Nevada and doing silver mining for the Cash Box Mining Company.

In May of 1922 Ivan married Frances Hodge in Cascada, a community in Fresno County, California (located in the High Sierras). It is mentioned that he was a successful proprietor in the county. In August of 1925 a Las Vegas Age article reports that former resident Ivan and his wife Frances were seriously injured in a car accident. They were on their way home from Huntington Lake when their vehicle was hit by another car and rolled down a canyon. They survived.

By 1925 Ivan was a machinist in the Big Creek area of Fresno County in California. The 1930 Federal Census had him mining in the Hot Creek region in Nye County, Nevada.

As the Great Depression progressed in the early 1930's, Ivan found himself unemployed. After two years of being unable to support his wife, Frances in 1932 filed for divorce in Reno. She went on to waitress in Fresno where she lived out her life.

Ivan fell ill in late 1939 and spent the final 14 months of his life in a hospital. He died on December 26, 1940, from lung disease related to his mining days. He was buried in Tonopah, Nevada on January 6, 1941.

Ivan Botkin played a small but interesting role in the early developmental days of Las Vegas.

Chapter 8
JOHN WISNER AND THE OVERLAND HOTEL

Two of the nicest early hotels to grace Las Vegas were constructed within 18 months after the auction of town lots by the railroad was completed. John F. Miller would open the Hotel Nevada at the southeast corner of Main and Fremont while John S. Wisner would build his Overland Hotel at the northeast corner. Both were just across Main Street from the train depot. Arriving train passengers now had two nice hotels to choose from. The competition for guests was on.

John Stewart Wisner was born January 27, 1856, in Valparaiso, Indiana. His parents were Daniel "Clinton" Wisner (1819-1873) and Phoebe Protzman Wisner (1829-1866). Clinton was a farmer. They were married in 1847 in Indiana. John Wisner had four siblings -- Frank (1848-1919), Daniel (1849-1939), Silas (1852-1928), and Willard (1861-1942). The Wisner family had lineage going back to the colonial days of New York.

It is believed that John headed west with his father in 1871 and it is known that they were living in New Mexico in 1879. John became a contractor and by the early 1880's was doing jobs for a variety of railroads in western states. In January 1887 he married Anna ("Annie") Rosaria ("Rosa") Hitchcock, age 22, in Kittitas County within the Washington Territory. Annie was raising two young boys from a prior marriage. In the late 1800's John Wisner worked on projects as a railroad contractor for the Great Northern Railroad. He helped complete the first rail tunnels through a mountain (the Northern Pacific Tunnel and the Horseshoe Tunnel through the Cascades). John and Annie had one child together, a girl named Lillian "Ethel", born in Oregon in March of 1888. In the 1890's the Wisner family was residing in Tacoma, Washington.

John Wisner's daughter Ethel and his wife Annie are in the rear of this circa 1900 family photo.
Ancestry.org

In November of 1900 Annie was granted a divorce from John on the grounds of "abandonment and failure to provide". John did not contest the divorce and Annie received full custody of their daughter. Annie and Ethel remained in Tacoma.

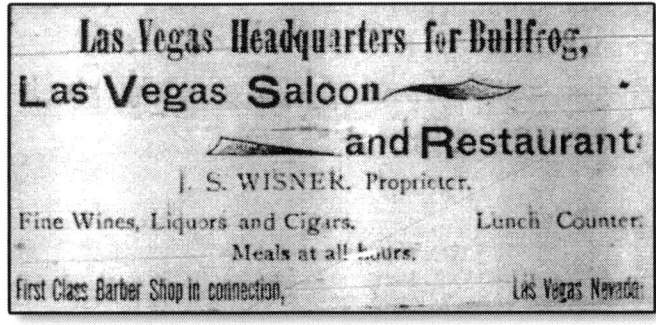
June 3, 1905, Las Vegas Times ad

John landed a contract from the San Pedro, Los Angeles, and Salt Lake Railroad company in 1904 to work on their line connecting Southern California to Las Vegas. That brought him to the barren Las Vegas area.

Wisner's name shows up as having purchased a number of lots in McWilliams' Original Townsite. He quickly established a small saloon and restaurant on Railroad Street that also housed a Kramer brother barber shop.

Rare early 1906 postcard photo. The Overland Hotel is seen on the left.

John Wisner's first hotel structure, which he called the Overland Hotel, was built on the east side of Main Street between Fremont and Ogden, just south of the alley that ran down the middle of Block 2. It was open by early July 1905 and housed an adjacent business called the Overland Cafe which was run by Charles Wing.

July 22, 1905, Las Vegas Times ad

July 22, 1905, Las Vegas Age ad for Wing's Overland Cafe

John's hotel interior was said to be of corrugated red iron. That summer John volunteered to serve on a committee comprised of businessmen to raise funds for a volunteer fire department.

In 1905 Wisner teamed with partners to establish claims in the Crescent Mining District. By 1906 they were successful in hitting large veins of silver ore that fetched them $48 per ton.

A year after the land auction, the northeast corner lots of Main and Fremont still sat vacant. Wisner obtained possession of those lots and in late August of 1906 announced plans to build an addition (30 by 50 feet) to his current hotel so it would reach closer to Fremont Street. He planned to build a two-story structure with 20 large bedrooms that would be attached to the south side of his existing hotel. His original hotel would house a kitchen and dining room and serve as a wing of his new building. It opened before the end of 1906. John hoped his cafe would appeal to visiting hungry miners.

John added a stone block front to his addition in December of 1906 and by mid-May of 1907 he had finished installing a veranda along the second floor on Main Street. With his corner lots having 25 feet of frontage on Main and depths of 140 feet parallel to Fremont, John had ample space along Fremont to continue adding on to his hotel. So, in September of 1907 he announced that he would add 75 feet to his hotel along Main (to reach the corner) and another 40 feet to wrap it around the corner onto Fremont. It was an $8,000 project that would be two stories in height. When done the veranda would encircle the entire second floor. The new portions of the lower floor would house a bar, dining room, wine room, kitchen and pantry. Upstairs would be the new bedrooms, shared baths and a ladies parlor. Work was done quickly and before the end of 1907 the new addition was done and John announced his property would offer a new cafe, gaming and liquor. Even though the railroad had restricted the sale of alcohol to Blocks 16 and 17, the early hotels were successful in getting around the regulation.

Electric lights were added to the entire veranda in 1908 to illuminate it at night. In May of 1909 John remodeled the hotel's office and did some general improvements.

April 4, 1909, Las Vegas Age ad. For years, Wisner would have an ad in every edition of the Age with a photo of his hotel and a list of all newly arriving guests beneath it

Over the years ahead John continued to lease out his bar and cafe to many different people. In June of 1909 F.E. Matzdorf (age 50) became the new manager of the Overland Cafe. He had run an eatery in Los Angeles in 1903 and later in 1906 was headed to Goldfield when he decided to take a detour and check out Las Vegas. He took a chance and stayed. After signing his lease, Matzdorf painted and decorated the cafe. He reopened it for business on June 6, 1909. In December of 1909 Wisner leased his Overland Bar to Merritt Pollard of Los Angeles.

Photo circa 1911 of the Overland Hotel

New cement sidewalks went in on Main and Fremont in front of the Overland Hotel in April of 1910.

Vendors would often sell fruit and vegetables to visitors by setting up carts on the side of the hotel on Main Street.

In January of 1911 Wisner made plans to add another 30 rooms to his hotel. Work began in February to add a 60-foot hotel annex on Fremont. On the ground floor would be three storefronts while the upstairs portion would have the new bedrooms, baths and a space to show motion pictures. The first leased store to open along Fremont was the Red Front Store which began business by April. In May the upstairs veranda was extended along Fremont.

Just after 11 p.m. on May 23, 1911, tragedy struck. A fire broke out in Matzdorf's kitchen that soon jumped to the veranda. It spread quickly and engulfed most of the now 100 by 60-foot Overland Hotel. Sleeping guests had virtually no

Produce cart from nearby Kiel Ranch. Photo circa 1911.
UNLV Libraries, Special Collections

time to gather their possessions before fleeing. A railroad laborer was burned to death in his room and his body taken to the town's morgue run by E. W. Griffith. Residents of the Hotel Nevada across the street were alerted but luckily the fire did not spread beyond the Overland complex. Pollard and his new partner O'Neill were able to salvage some stock from their bar but suffered a $1200 loss. Matzdorf's Overland Cafe was a total loss. The almost brand new Red Front Store had an $11,000 loss in clothing, shoes and fixtures. Wisner's losses were placed at $25,000 and guests estimated their losses at $2,000. The fire made the young town focus more on improving their volunteer fire department.

May 27, 1911, Las Vegas Age newspaper headline about the Overland Hotel fire

Most of the Overland Hotel and its storefronts were destroyed in the fire
UNLV Libraries, Special Collections

Wisner collected only $6500 in insurance money and announced he would rebuild his hotel quickly. It would again be two-stories but concrete and fireproof. The Red Front Store received $3000 from their insurance claim and opened a temporary store elsewhere while waiting for Wisner to rebuild. Pollard and O'Neill also found a temporary spot for their bar. Matzdorf went to Los Angeles on a vacation after announcing he would run his restaurant for a few months inside the Nevada Meat Market.

The clearing of debris began in early July and by the end of the month the rebuild had commenced. The new structure would have 30 rooms, some with private baths. Matzdorf decided not to return and John Leighton of Rhyolite made plans to lease the new cafe when it was ready to open. With the second floor almost done in November, a severe wind storm damaged the new roof slightly delaying the opening of the hotel. So some six months after the fire occurred, the Overland Hotel was back in business on November 18, 1911.

Las Vegas Age photo in late 1911 showing how the rebuilt Overland Hotel appeared before Wisner added back the veranda

O'Neill decided to retire and Pollard took over as sole proprietor of the bar. In December of 1911 Leighton transferred his lease of the cafe to Paul Buol, a brother of Las Vegas' first mayor.

A panoramic photo circa 1912 showing the distance disembarking train passengers had to walk from the depot to Main and Fremont. The Overland Hotel is seen just to the right of center.

In March of 1912 Wisner began adding back the wrap-around veranda to make his new hotel resemble the old one. It would offer sun protection for guests. New sidewalks went in during March of 1912. In June the hotel's restaurant was taken over by George Bergman.

In February of 1913 when Wisner lost the key to the front door of the hotel, he made the decision to remain open day and night. In October of 1913, John's daughter Ethel came to town to visit after having spent the prior 18 months in San Diego. November 1913 saw yet new owners of the Overland Cafe -- Fred Weaverling and E.H. Ferguson.

In January of 1914 Wisner added new plate glass windows on the first floor along Fremont. In May the hotel got a barbershop run by Ed Walters from Montana. During the summer of 1915 Julius Fox leased the cafe and advertised 50-cent chicken dinners. By the end of the year Fox was gone and two experienced caterers (Coleman & Kelly) took over running the cafe. They installed a long new lunch counter.

In January of 1916 Wisner became the 2nd Vice-President of the Las Vegas Chamber of Commerce. That summer his hotel was granted an actual liquor license by the county. In October of 1917 a new hand laundry and dry cleaning operation came to the Overland Hotel. That November Wisner leased the entire property to William E. Arnold and his partner Clinton.

A hotel token issued by Overland Hotel proprietors Arnold & Clinton

The swinging western style doors can be seen at the entrance to the Overland Hotel in this circa 1918 photo
UNLV Libraries, Special Collections

The gentlemen made plans to remodel the entire front of the building as well as the interior lobby and bar. With World War I in progress, sacrifices were made to support the war effort as the cafe went meatless on Tuesdays and wheat free on Wednesdays. In December of 1917 Meritt Pollard ended his 8-year lease of the Overland Bar and moved across the street to run the competing Hotel Nevada Bar.

Early January 1918 saw some remodeling done to the hotel. A corner room to house the bar and a cigar stand was completed and the front entrance was removed and replaced with large plate glass windows along with double swinging doors. The lobby also received upgrading.

Wisner obtained approval to add a 60 by 40-foot concrete garage on Main Street which was completed in April, 1918. One S.B. Christian became the new manager of the cafe. Wisner spent April and May vacationing in San Francisco and Seattle. When liquor sales were prohibited in town in late 1918, the Overland Bar was repurposed as an amusement area.

In October of 1919 John completed construction on a small concrete building in the rear of the hotel to serve as his office. It also had a space to park his car. In May of 1920 he went on an extended two-month trip to Los Angeles and then the east coast. He planned to return by way of Detroit where he would buy himself a new vehicle to drive home. In November he converted his garage on Main Street to create a few more rooms to rent. He thought of adding a third floor on to the Overland Hotel but decided to wait until construction costs decreased. In November of 1920 Wisner signed a three-year lease of the Overland Hotel with W. P. Bressingham of Salt Lake City after proprietor Arnold had serious health issues. It would begin on January 1, 1921. A jitney service operating out of the hotel began in December which offered to transport folks "anywhere, anytime". Bressingham did some remodeling, adding 12 rooms on Main Street and turned the bar area into a place for soft drinks. He travelled to Salt Lake City to purchase linens for the newly added rooms.

In early 1922 Wisner fell ill with heart trouble and spent several days in the hospital. Afterwards he returned to his hotel to rest. That June he headed to Puget Sound in Washington and then to Los Angeles on a long vacation. While in Los Angeles he died on June 28 in his Biltmore Hotel room. The cause was attributed to cirrhosis of the liver and heart disease. He was 66 years old at the time and was buried in an Inglewood, California cemetery.

Wisner's grave marker
Find A Grave website

The hotel and his estate valued at around $100,000 (in addition to $8000 per year in generated lease income) went to his daughter Ethel who at the time was residing in Banning, California and married to man named Gus Genther.

Undated photo of Ethel Wisner
Ancestry.org

Ethel asked her uncle Lou Hitchcock to come and manage the hotel. In October of 1923 he had a new roof installed and rooms were plastered and painted to make them look brighter. In addition, the rooms received new furniture and rugs and a florist store opened. In January of 1924 a San Francisco eye specialist set up shop in leased space for three weeks. The next month saw Ethel and Gus build a new lobby for the hotel with a nice staircase. The old lobby became a barber shop along with space for a cigar stand and soft drink sales. They also purchased new bedding for the hotel rooms. The city had recently paved Fremont Street from Main to 5th Street which helped local businesses. In April Ethel signed a long-term lease with her uncle so he could run the hotel. Her health was not the best and she went to California to rest for seven months. Uncle Lou leased the bar space to C. Fenner, W.E. Nolan and J.L. McLaurine on April 15. Later that year Ethel went to Los Angeles and took up residence there.

In April of 1925 E.A. Beckett subleased the hotel and installed a cigar and confectionary stand. He quickly transferred the lease to M.E. McDermott of Hollywood who had experience running hotels in Utah and Wyoming. The cafe was being run by W.P. Gilbreath who added on a dining room. Seven months later the restaurant was under the control of a John Van Ryn. Early 1926 saw stores on Fremont receive addresses as the post office initiated direct delivery of mail. In 1926 the Overland Hotel housed the Montello Shoe Shop, but it moved that summer over to Hotel Nevada. In late 1926 the Las Vegas Real Estate Co. opened up in the former cafe dining room.

Hotel operator Beckett was not able to keep pace with demands for room rentals by business travelers. So in June of 1927 he leased the Wilson Hotel to the south of the Overland Hotel on Main Street (at Stewart). It was under construction at the time and 38 of its 71 rooms were already completed. In November he was able to buy the Wilson Hotel and made plans to add on a third floor to it.

In February of 1928 Beckett ended his lease of the Overland Hotel and went on to the Union Hotel at Main and Bridger. Helen signed a new lease with R.A. Ashtenhagen of California who had many years of experience running hotels. He put in new heating and furnishings. In late April of 1928 a Mr. Free took over the cafe and in November it was renamed the Manhattan Cafe.

It received new fixtures and a modern kitchen. It was operated by a Mr. G. Kapotas.

August 21, 1931, Las Vegas Review Journal ad

A photo taken in the late 1920's of the Overland Hotel
*UNLV Libraries, Special Collections;
Elton & Madelaine Garret Photo Collection (0265 0215)*

In September of 1928 the first neon sign in Las Vegas was installed over the entrance of the Overland Hotel
Photo courtesy of historian Robert Stoldal

In January of 1929 Thomas S. Carroll opened up a real estate office in the hotel along Fremont Street. A dedicated showroom for traveling vendors was established on the second floor. In March of 1930 Ethel came to Las Vegas for a visit. She was accompanied by her mother and her maternal grandmother, P. A. Hitchcock. They took up residence at 718 S. 4th Street.

When Ashtenhagen's three-year lease ended in February of 1931 Ethel took over as manager of the hotel. Later that month her grandmother died in one of the hotel's rooms. She was 84 and was possibly one of the first white females to be born in the Oregon Territory (1847). That summer the Overland Barber Shop moved into 8 Fremont Street.

June 6, 1931, Review Journal ad

December 9, 1931, Review Journal ad

April 18, 1932, Review Journal ad

In late 1931 the Davis Jewelry store opened in one of the hotel's storefronts on Fremont.

In April of 1932 a new two-story 100-foot-long garage was completed by Ethel just north of the hotel at 109 No. Main St. It was leased to

January 26, 1933, Review Journal ad

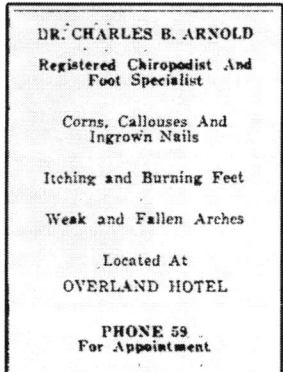

Foot doctor ad in the December 1, 1932, Review Journal

December 4, 1934, Review Journal ad

December 24, 1932, Review Journal ad

June 13, 1935, Review Journal ad

James Cashman for a car showroom (Buicks and Pontiacs), a repair space and an office. Upstairs he had room to store tires and parts. In May Cashman's garage was enlarged and the hotel received a larger lobby and a new cooling system. Also in April, Jackson's Cafe opened up for business.

During the summer of 1932 the Overland Stage Line started operating out of the hotel. It offered nine-hour bus rides to Los Angeles on the two lane road out of town. Unfortunately, its buses had no air conditioning. (The company later became the Interstate Transit Lines and left the hotel in 1942; it went on to become Greyhound.) Other stage lines over the years operated ticket offices in the Overland Hotel.

In September of 1932 the cafe came under the ownership of Myrtle Holberg and Betty Dieleman. Ethel had apparently taken up residence in Los Angeles once again. By the end of 1932 the new Savoy Cafe was operating in the hotel.

As one can see, the hotel's cafe and bar went through numerous changes in name and proprietors over the decades. Like the Hotel Nevada, the Overland Hotel was often used by many travelling medical practitioners to set up temporary offices to offer their needed services to local residents.

By the early 1930's Ethel was now married to a Mr. J. Buren Evans. He used to be a miner in Ivanpah, Nevada.

In December of 1934 the Vegas Art Shop was in business at 8 Fremont Street.

In the summer of 1935 A.M. Wheeler became the new manager of the Overland Hotel.

Ethel and her husband now had a summer home in Walport, Oregon with their main residence being in Reno. In November the Sun Drug Co. took over 10 Fremont Street. By the mid-30's the old roof top signs had been taken down.

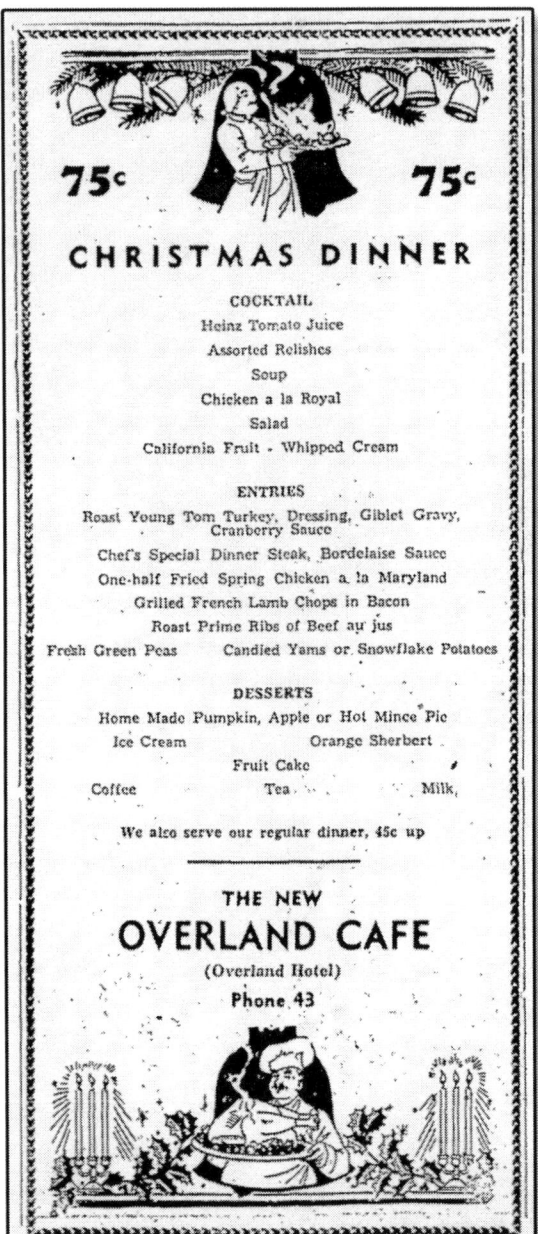

December 23, 1939, Review Journal ad

Late 1930's photo of the hotel with its new arched sign
Vintage Las Vegas website photo

In January of 1937 an arched "Overland" sign was installed on the Fremont Street side of the hotel.

In November the hotel received a little remodeling with Mr. and Mrs. Peter Clos serving as new managers. 1939 saw the "New Overland Cafe" open.

Ethel would visit occasionally on business over the years ahead.

It was in June of 1945 when Ethel decided to sell the Overland Hotel.

Ray Salmon of Ogden purchased it for around $275,000. He was a hotel operator and stockman in Utah. The hotel had 53 rooms and four apartments. It had about 100 feet of frontage on Fremont (cafe, bar, stores) and 180 feet on Main which included Cashman's car operation. Salmon leased out the hotel bar to Sid Martin.

May 31, 1945, Review Journal ad

December 31, 1945, Review Journal ad

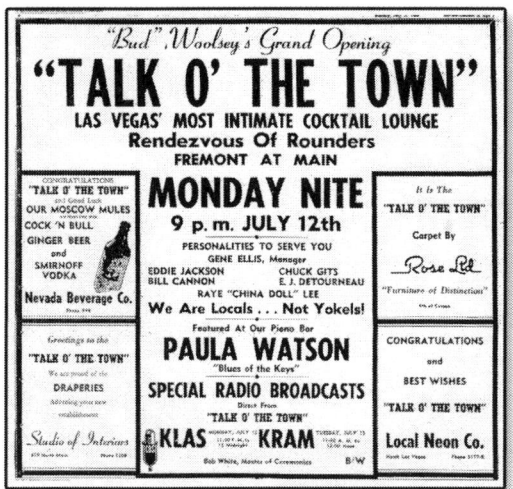

July 11, 1948, Review Journal ad

Photo circa 1947 showing the large new hotel sign that included a train locomotive
Courtesy of the Clark County Museum

In 1946 Salmon installed a massive three-ton neon sign on the hotel. It was an incredible 28 feet tall and showed an old-time steam engine spouting smoke as it hauled coaches behind it.

In July of 1948 the "Talk O' the Town" lounge was opened by Bud Wolsey in the hotel.

Salmon took on a partner, a Mr. J. Kell Houssels, and they enlarged the bar giving it a Western motif. Houssels had been operating the Las Vegas Club across the street at 21 Fremont Street since 1930. They then leased the hotel operation to the Continental Hotel System. In 1949 Houssels remodeled the entire lower floor of the building and moved in his Las Vegas Club from across the street. Sometime in the late 1940's or early 1950's new Spanish-style stone shingles went up on the roof.

In 1953 "The Chatterbox" lounge replaced the "Talk O' the Town" and a few years later turned into "Biffs". The old balcony on the second floor along Fremont came down to make way for new neon signage for Biffs and the Las Vegas Club.

Photo by author

In early 1961 Jackie Gaughan and Mel Exber purchased the hotel. The entire Overland property was sold to the Las Vegas Club for just over one million dollars in May of 1962. The original Overland Hotel name was dropped in the mid-1960's. The Las Vegas Club remodeled the casino in 1978 and a tower was added on in 1980. Another tower of rooms came in 1996 bringing the hotel to 410 rooms. The hotel sold to Barrick Gaming in 2004 and in 2005 went to the Tamares Group. The hotel was closed in April of 2013 and the entire property was purchased by Greg and Derek Stevens in August 2015. The casino closed in August of 2015 and the Stevens brothers began demolishing in 2017 the entire city block between Fremont and Ogden from Main to 1st Street. They built a mega-resort property geared towards adults called the Circa. The casino portion opened in October of 2020 and the hotel two months later.

If you visit the impressive Circa property, be sure to take a look back at the early photos of John Wisner's original Overland Hotel from well over a century earlier. What a difference time and money can make.

John's widow Annie passed away at age 88 in St. Petersburg, Florida in 1954. John's daughter Ethel passed away in October of 1978 at age 90. Unfortunately, no photos of John S. Wisner could be found. The Overland Hotel had a long and illustrious run and proudly served thousands of guests visiting early Las Vegas. It was a prominent downtown landmark for many decades.

Chapter 9
John Miller and the Hotel Nevada

John Miller would open his impressive Hotel Nevada in January of 1906 and by the end of that year John Wisner had completed his large expansion of the Overland Hotel directly across the street. The two hotels would remain competitors for decades to come.

A photo of Fremont Street looking east from Main Street circa 1920 showing how the Overland Hotel on the left and Hotel Nevada on the right were very close to each other
Courtesy of the Nevada State Museum, Las Vegas

A circa mid-1906 photo showing the two-story Hotel Nevada in the center and the original smaller Overland Hotel (before its expansion) off to the left
Courtesy of the Nevada State Museum, Las Vegas

Only located photo of John Miller. Taken in November of 1936 at age 72.
UNLV Libraries, Special Collections; Elbert Edwards Photo Collection (0214 0574)

John Franklin Miller (born August 3, 1864, in Indiana) was one of the early pioneers who arrived on the first train in from California and secured a bed in Ladd's tent hotel. He was a saloon and hotel operator from the Santa Barbara area of California and was 40 years old. With a train car positioned just west of the intersection of Main Street and Fremont Street serving as a temporary depot, it was only natural that the most desirable lots to be auctioned off were in that general area. John Miller obtained a row of nine lots on the east side of Main Street commencing south from the corner at Fremont Street. Each lot was 25 feet wide on Main Street and 140 feet deep (paralleling Fremont). He set up a temporary canvas and wood tent hotel which he called "Hotel Nevada" on one of his lots. He could not build a permanent structure until Kuhn Mercantile moved off the corner of Main and Fremont.

With Norman Kuhn's general store gone by September of 1905, Miller was able to begin excavation work for the cellar and foundation of a two-story concrete hotel. It would have 65 feet of frontage on Main and 40 feet on Fremont with a 10-foot-wide alley in the rear.

John made arrangements for water to be brought in and construction of the lower level began in late September. Work on the second floor began in late October. Before the project was completed, John decided to add 60 additional feet along Fremont that would blend into what was already built. The ground floor along Fremont and Main was designed to house numerous businesses with depths of 65 feet. The second floor would contain rooms for boarders. Space upstairs was also set aside for leasing to lodges. Hotel Nevada was called the "Queen of the Desert" in one of the local newspapers.

September 1905 newspaper ad for Miller's tent hotel

Photo of initial phase of Hotel Nevada in 1905 just before expansion got underway. Hotel Nevada had no signage at this time.

In January of 1906 all work was completed, and Hotel Nevada opened on January 13 as the first concrete hotel in Southern Nevada.

With gambling legal in Nevada, Miller was quick to add space devoted to gaming. John was proud that his 35 hotel rooms (which each measured 10 feet by 10 feet) had electrical lights, steam radiators, hot and cold water, indoor plumbing and were well ventilated. It was a first-class hotel property. Rooms went for $1 per night.

Photo circa 1908 of the Hotel Nevada with its Fremont Street expansion now completed and signage installed
Courtesy of the Nevada State Museum, Las Vegas

The railroad had set aside only two blocks (16 and 17) in their town where alcohol could be sold. Hotel Nevada was in Block 3. Nevertheless, when the Overland Hotel began serving alcohol, Hotel Nevada followed along. A leased restaurant (which was merely a long bar which served lunches) was opened and like with the Overland Hotel, over time they would change proprietors many times. In its early days, Miller's hotel was earning more revenue from gambling and alcohol than from its rooms.

Over the years ahead the hotel lobby, offices, entrance and store fronts underwent many renovations. The businesses along Fremont and Main would house a wide variety of merchants from 1905 on. The stores would become home to a barber shop, a tailor, a men's clothing store, numerous cafes, a cigar stand, a shoe shop, a Maytag store, a taxi service, a bank, a bakery, a drug store, a realtor, a confectionary shop and many others. Visiting doctors, dentists, and optometrists would periodically lease space to serve the needs of the town's citizens.

John Miller continued to own a hotel back in Summerland, California (a suburb of Santa Barbara) and had interests in oil fields there as well. In September of 1906 he had claims in the Vincent Mining District which was southeast of Las Vegas.

In April 1906 cement sidewalks went in along the Main Street side of the hotel. Miller did a small 20 by 20 foot addition to his hotel in late 1906 to add on a kitchen with four more bedrooms above. During the summer of 1907 John installed metal ceilings in the bar, office and dining room. When local phone service came to Las Vegas in June of 1907, a phone was placed in the hotel's cigar store and received phone number 1. With the hotel doing well, John purchased a big new safe for the office. In 1908 he further expanded his hotel by 60 feet along Fremont, again matching the old structure's appearance. That summer John volunteered to serve on a committee (The Lincoln County Division Club) along with other leading citizens to discuss a possible breakaway from Lincoln County to form what would become Clark County in 1909.

Replica of the original hotel phone on display for public viewing inside today's Golden Gate Casino

Sometime in 1908 Miller purchased land in Paradise Valley eight miles south of town to start a ranch. In 1909 he had a number of successful artesian wells drilled and brought in from California a carload of farming items (tools, wagons, seeds, and mules). In late 1908 he organized a corporation called the Nevada Hotel Mining Company that would control all his holdings -- his operations and land in California, his lots in Las Vegas, his Nevada ranch and mining interests, and his Hotel Nevada. John served as the company's manager.

When Nevada banned gambling in 1909 (with an effective date of late September 1910), John was forced to cease his gaming enterprise. All gambling items had to be moved into storage. Also in 1909, awnings were installed above the windows on the second floor along the Fremont side of the hotel. Soon after, the Main Street side of the hotel would receive pillars that would support a second-floor balcony.

Photo circa 1910 showing awnings on the second floor along Fremont Street and a balcony running along the Main Street side

A 1911 photo of Hotel Nevada's Main Street side. Off on the left can be seen repair work to the Overland Hotel storefronts after its 1911 fire
Courtesy of Vicki Carnes whose grandfather Ed McGriff took the photo

June 17, 1911, Las Vegas Age ad

Photo circa 1912 of Hotel Nevada. Stores on the Fremont side include a restaurant with bakery, a barbershop, and a men's clothing store. The hotel's dining room sign can be seen to the right along Main Street.
UNLV Libraries, Special Collections

In 1910 Miller had 40 acres under cultivation on his ranch with six employees plus a cabin and a barn. He was growing wheat, oats, barley, and alfalfa. An irrigation system was installed. Cattle were brought in and branded. In August of 1910 at age 46, John began to feel exhausted and decided to take time off to visit California and then his Nevada ranch to rest. He resigned his managerial position at the hotel and George Carlin took over temporary control of the hotel until he returned. John extended his time away from the hotel and leased it out to others to run over the next few years.

By early 1914 John was back in control of his hotel and had become a member of the Clark County Farm Bureau. In March of 1914 a ten-foot-wide cement sidewalk went in along the hotel on Fremont Street.

In February of 1918 John agreed to accept an appointment to the Las Vegas City Commission to fill a vacancy. He was placed in charge of the city's police and fire departments. That year the Spanish Flu was underway. John was stricken but survived. He ended his service as a city commissioner in June of 1919.

In early 1922 a new bank was formed in Las Vegas and was housed along Fremont Street in Hotel Nevada. John was one of the founders of the "Bank of Southern Nevada" and served as its president. (It was closed on December 31, 1933, during the Great Depression after having been deemed no longer profitable.)

In the early 1920's Miller built a garage structure on his remaining empty lots (along Main Street and south of his hotel) that he leased out to an auto repair shop. In 1925 the city paved Fremont Street. When mail delivery to homes and businesses in Las Vegas was established in 1926, street addresses were assigned and Hotel Nevada received 1 Fremont Street.

In April of 1927 Miller added a final 40 feet of frontage to his hotel on Fremont Street that brought the hotel to its full extension to the alleyway in the middle of the block. It created space for three more stores and a lunchroom.

In September of 1929 John put his 440-acre ranch south of town up for sale. He said it had 100 acres of alfalfa, 9 wells, and fencing. It would take many years for him to find a buyer with the Great Depression in progress. (Eventually his ranch would become today's Sunset Park.)

Rhodes Auto Garage can be seen on the far right along Main Street in this undated photo. On the side of the hotel along Fremont Street can be seen a sign for the Bank of Southern Nevada.
UNLV Libraries, Special Collections

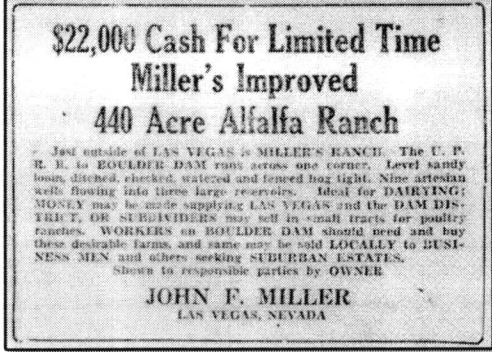

April 18, 1931, Las Vegas Age ad

December 3, 1931, Las Vegas Age ad for Hotel Nevada

In 1930 John became the vice-president of the "Greater Las Vegas Club" that was formed by local businessmen to promote the city and the upcoming Boulder Dam.

Another story was added to Hotel Nevada in 1931 that would bring several dozen more rooms to the hotel.

Postcard circa 1933 of Hotel Sal Sagev
Vintage Las Vegas website

Ad with Hotel Sagev rates published in the 1931 Las Vegas City Directory

When legalized gambling returned to Nevada in 1931 (to stimulate business and job growth during the Great Depression) the casino returned and the hotel commenced plans to change its name to Sal Sagev (Las Vegas spelled backwards). A large neon hotel name sign was attached to the building in the spring of 1932. It was over 30 feet tall and each letter measured 6 feet by 4 feet.

1940's photo of Fremont Street looking east from Main Street. Overland Hotel is on the left and Hotel Sal Sagev on the right.
Courtesy of the Nevada State Museum, Las Vegas

Souvenir menu for a $3.50 Sal Sagev Dining Room 1948 Thanksgiving multi-course meal.
UNLV Libraries, Special Collections

In the late 1930's Miller started a large ranch in northwest Arizona. In 1938 he built a $250,000 thirty-unit auto court and gas station called El Trovatore Arizona Autel Court in the Kingman area of Arizona. In 1940 he doubled it in size. His daughter helped manage the property. A Las Vegas newspaper also reported Miller had large ranch holdings in Canada.

In July of 1940 Miller served as secretary of the Clark County General Public Hospital Board. In 1942 he was appointed a member of the Nevada State Defense Advisory Committee that sold bonds to support our World War II efforts.

During the summer of 1945 John had an accident on his Arizona ranch that broke a vertebrae and put him in a body cast for a number of months. By the late 1940's, now in his 80's, John retired from hotel and civic work in Las Vegas. His son Abe was already managing the Sal Sagev.

Cemetery marker for John F. Miller
Billion Graves website

John still oversaw his Arizona ranch and auto court while living in an apartment in his hotel. The last five years of his life John was in declining health. He died in his sleep in his room on February 13, 1957, at the age of 92. John F. Miller was buried in Woodlawn Cemetery.

In July of 1955 son Abe Miller had leased the Sal Sagev's first floor to a large group of 23 investors. They in turn subleased the ground floor to eight Italian-American men (most of whom were from the Oakland, California area) who wished to open a casino. They agreed to pay Abe $2300 a month plus 5% of their net gambling profits. The men opened their property in October and they and their family members would manage the "Golden Gate Casino" for the next 40 years.

October 30, 1955, Las Vegas Review Journal ad

The casino used a San Francisco theme and in 1959 brought the shrimp cocktail (25-cents) to Las Vegas. The upstairs hotel kept the Sal Sagev name.

Photo circa 1957 of the Golden Gate Casino on the ground floor and Hotel Sal Sagev on the upper two floors
UNLV Libraries, Special Collections; Manis Photo Collection (0100 3448)

In the 1960's the casino was a frequent hangout for the members of the famous Rat Pack. The hotel portion was expanded to 106 rooms in 1964. Abe Miller and his sister Helen maintained control of the property. The entire property took on the name "Golden Gate Hotel and Casino" in 1974. After the deaths of Abe and Helen by the early 1980's, children of one of the casino operators were able to buy full interest in the property in 1990. The hotel portion had 106 rooms at the time. In 1995 the Fremont Street Experience put in a canopy for light shows over Fremont Street and closed the street to traffic from Main Street heading east to 4th Street.

Photo (by author) of the Golden Gate today with the Fremont Street Experience canopy above Fremont

Photo by author of the Golden Gate Casino and Hotel as seen from across Main Street

The hotel/casino structure was renovated in 2005 by then owner Mark Brandenburg. In March of 2008 he sold half interest in the property to Derek and Greg Stevens of Desert Rock Enterprises. Hotel rooms were improved and the casino upgraded. In 2006 the Stevens increased their ownership to 60%. Derek became CEO and Brandenburg assumed the role of President. In 2012 the Golden Gate underwent a major $12 million renovation project which added on a hotel tower. The Stevens brothers succeeded in becoming full owners of the property in 2016. In August of 2017 the casino floor doubled in size. Today the Golden Gate remains a vibrant hotel and casino on Fremont Street.

This chapter concludes with some discussion about John Miller's family history. Mother Anna had 8 children with husband Daniel who was a farmer. Daniel died young in 1874. At some point Anna moved the family to California. In 1914 at about age 89 she visited her son John in Las Vegas. At the time of her death, she was survived by just four of her eight children.

Undated photo of a young Adah Nosser
Ancestry.org

Grave marker for Adah Laura Miller
Find A Grave

John F. Miller was married twice and had seven children. His first wife was Adah Laura Nosser Miller who gave him five children. She was born in 1871 in Nebraska and died in 1964 in the Santa Barbara area of California. It is not known exactly when or where they were married.

Their first child, John Jr., was born in 1889 and passed in 1976 in California. He was a farmer and had a daughter who was born in 1930.

Their second child was Benjamin "Franklin" Miller born in 1896. He was a married road laborer who later in life lived in southern Arizona. He died in San Diego County in 1993.

Child number three was Opal Miller Lambert who was born in 1898. She and her husband resided in the Summerland area, a community about five miles east of Santa Barbara. It was apparently the location where John Miller lived before moving to Las Vegas in the early 1900's. Opal passed in 1997.

The fourth child was Harry W. Miller who was born in 1899. He was a farmer and handyman who married Myrtle Isabelle White in 1945. Harry passed away in 1978 in Summerland.

Adah and John's final child was Daniel Albert Miller. He was born in 1902 and was an electrician. It is not known when he died.

In Las Vegas Adah served as Hotel Nevada's clerk. She divorced John on grounds of desertion in May of 1911 and returned to Summerland, California to run the Summerland Hotel. She received $6,000 along with other property in Summerland. John got to keep his hotel and ranch in Nevada as well as all other properties and investments he had.

John did not wait long to remarry. Some five months later in September of 1911 he married Rosa C. Marchetti in New Jersey. She was born in Italy on August 1, 1884 and was 20 years younger than he was. She passed in Kingman, Arizona in August of 1962 at age 78 and was buried in Woodlawn by her husband. She did give John two children.

Woodlawn Cemetery grave marker for Rosa Miller
Find A Grave

February 6, 1958,
Las Vegas Review Journal
photo of Abe Miller

Their first child was Abraham ("Abe") Miller. He was born on August 19, 1912. He graduated Las Vegas High School in 1930 and went on to attend Northwestern University where he played football. After graduating college in 1936 he returned to Las Vegas and began working in his father's hotel as a restaurant manager. In the 1940's he assumed a greater role in operating the hotel.

His wife Linnea bore him a son and two daughters. From the late 1950's to May of 1964 Abe served on the Nevada State Planning Board. After selling his interest in the hotel, Abe relocated the family to Sedona, Arizona where he helped open an art center. It was called The Tlaquepaque Complex and was built from materials that were brought in from Mexico. Abe dabbled in real estate and built both a Ramada Inn and a shopping center in Flagstaff. He spent the final 10 years of his life in Sedona, dying there in March of 1982 at age 69. He left behind three children and seven grandchildren, all living in Sedona.

Grave marker in Woodlawn Cemetery for Abe Miller
Find A Grave

Woodlawn Cemetery marker for Helen Miller Nugent
Find A Grave

John's seventh child, and second one with Rosa, was Helen R. Miller Nugent born in Las Vegas in 1915. She was married multiple times and lived for some time in Reno in the 1940's where she and a husband operated a cleaning store. After father John's death in 1957 she helped her brother Abe run the hotel for a few months until it was leased. She passed on June 29, 1979, at age 64.

Hotel Nevada served an important role in the development of Las Vegas. Thousands of early arrivers spent time there over the early decades of Las Vegas as the city grew. The many businesses housed on the ground floor of the hotel served the varied needs of town residents. John Miller was active in civic affairs and social groups. He was a long-time participant and supporter of the Chamber of Commerce. He was also a charter member of the Elks Lodge and Kiwanis Club. He was definitely a noteworthy early Las Vegas pioneer. Remarkably, John Miller's original hotel structure still stands at Fremont and Main Streets well over a century later!

Photos of a two-sided aluminum token that John Miller commissioned to advertise his new hotel and its amenities.

Chapter 10
Jake and Will Beckley
Merchants

Two of the more interesting early arriving Las Vegas pioneers were brothers Jake and William Beckley. Jake arrived in 1905 and Will followed in 1908. Both were born in Switzerland and were raised in Illinois. Will would become a long-time operator of a men's furnishings store and Jake would be involved in the lumber business, farming, and working for his brother in sales.

Jake and Will were two of seven children born to Henry and Magdelina Beckley in the second half of the nineteenth century in Switzerland. The parents were both born in 1841 and they married in 1868. Father Henry was in the lumber business. Their children were Henry Jr. (1869), John (1870), Emma (1871), Conrad (1873), Jake (1875), Will (1877), and Elizabeth (1878).

Will Beckley is on the left and brother Jake on the right in this circa 1909 photo
UNLV Libraries, Special Collections

The Beckley family arrived in the United States on May 22, 1884, and resided with the Von Tobel family in Fairbury, Illinois. The Von Tobel's were friends of theirs back in Switzerland. At the time Will was 6 and Jake about 8. Father Henry died in 1891 and mother Magdelina would eventually reside with some of her children in Illinois and Indiana. Jake dropped out of school so he could take on odd jobs to help provide for the family.

Photo of Will Beckley circa 1900 before he left for Los Angeles and then Las Vegas
UNLV Libraries, Special Collections

As a young man in the 1890's, Will worked as a clerk in his uncle George's clothing store in Illinois.

He also dabbled in farming. Brother Jake and good friend Ed Von Tobel felt Illinois was too cold for them. When they heard of a $30 one-way rail ticket to Los Angeles in 1903, they borrowed money and packed their bags. After arriving in Los Angeles, Jake would do barbering and Ed found work in a lumberyard.

In 1905 they saw an advertisement about the upcoming sale of lots in the newly forming railroad town of Las Vegas. They bought round-trip tickets on the first scheduled train to ever travel from Los Angeles to Las Vegas. Between them they only had about $100. They knew they couldn't afford to buy a choice lot as they would go for $750 or even higher. Nevertheless, they hopped on the train and attended the first day of the railroad's land auction on May 15, 1905. It was a very hot afternoon and they watched as many of the desirable lots were snapped up. On day two, enthusiasm had declined and some side street lots were going for much lower and fixed prices. The railroad was offering to rebate the price buyers paid for their railroad tickets to get to the auction. So, using what funds they had and cashing in on the ticket offer, they pooled their monies and purchased two less expensive lots on South 1st Street near Bridger. Unfortunately, Ed Von Tobel's lumberyard boss from Los Angeles was also bidding at the auction. After seeing Ed, he fired him. Ed and Jake would make Las Vegas their home.

Jake Beckley alongside a wagon load of lumber and grain being prepared for transport to the Bullfrog mining district. Undated photo.
UNLV Libraries, Special Collections

Ed started his own lumberyard after borrowing funds from his father (who was a major lumber operator in Illinois) for lumber, nails, hardware, and a horse and wagon. In November he would take on Jake as his partner. Initially, the early arrivers were seeking out cottonwood trees at the Old Stewart Ranch to use for lumber as there were few other alternatives. With demand great for lumber to build structures, they quickly had some seven competitors, including Ed's old boss from Los Angeles. Early on, Ed and Jake were barely making $50 each per month which was less than they were earning in Los Angeles. As the town grew and demand for lumber began to decrease, Ed was able to buy out two of his competitors. Their business was kept afloat by a demand for lumber and needed supplies by individuals and businesses in Rhyolite, Beatty, Bullfrog, Tonopah, Death Valley, Goodsprings and El Dorado Canyon.

In 1907 Ed and Jake started their own 120-acre ranch in the near barren Paradise Valley area around 8 miles south of the new town. In early 1908 Jake plowed about three acres to grow cereal, wheat, melons and plant vines. He would also add many eucalyptus trees and an orchard. By the end of the year the region had about a dozen ranches, each with their own artesian well. They would build a small cabin and take turns on Sundays taking care of the ranch.

Jake encouraged his brother Will to join him in Las Vegas. Will arrived from Illinois in March of 1908 with a bit under $1000 in his pockets. He opened a small men's clothing store near Main and Fremont Streets in a tent in which he also lived. He used his savings to purchase goods in Los Angeles to stock his business. To accumulate money Will did odd jobs and painted buildings, including Indian Reservation structures in Moapa for the federal government. He earned $5 per day painting. He also painted the Episcopal Church in town. Will lived in the rear of his store until 1910 to save money.

Will's clothing store is on the far left on the ground floor of Hotel Nevada in this 1912 photo
UNLV Libraries, Special Collections

In October of 1908 Will was able to lease space on Fremont Street for his business in the recently expanded Hotel Nevada on the southeast corner of Main and Fremont Streets. His store had nice fixtures and steel ceilings. He promised to sell only quality men's clothing and shoes. He stayed open 14 hours a day and business was light at first. The hotel building was in a prime location across the street from the train depot. New arrivals in town would mostly stay in the Hotel Nevada or the Overland Hotel across the street. Will's store was a good place for visitors to buy items they forgot to pack. In December he began offering tailor-made suits. He would regularly advertise in the local Las Vegas Age newspaper. Trousers were selling for between $1.75 and $5.

In June of 1909 brothers Will and Jake were able to make a trip to Indiana and Illinois to visit family. After returning, Will made a large purchase of new goods for his store and advertised a big sale to move out old merchandise.

In August of 1909, there was a fire that destroyed Ed and Jake's wooden ranch house resulting in a $150 loss.

In 1910 Will believed he had saved enough funds to marry. He proposed by mail to Leva Grimes, a teacher in Wolcott, Indiana. They were married on September 6, 1910, and returned to Las Vegas to live. Leva began working in Will's store and became very active in social circles. Over the decades ahead they would be regular participants in the many social clubs and groups which formed in Las Vegas. They would often entertain others at their home. The couple rented a home for $20 per month at 121 No. 4th Street from banker John S. Park. Will no longer had to live in his old tent.

In September Jake was serving as the local agent for a manufacturing company selling newly developed gas-powered well drilling rigs. He made money on the side drilling water wells.

Will's business was growing and in late 1911 he had a beautiful window display of Christmas goods. He purchased land with 90 feet of frontage on 4th Street, between Fremont and Carson, for $450 from Walter Bracken. He began building a four-room home in early 1912 and he and Leva moved in during the month of April in 1912. The home at 120 South 4th Street cost $2500 to construct. There was only one bedroom and their two soon-to-be born children would sleep in the attic. A Paiute woman was hired to help Leva with chores. Streetlights were not yet in, and Will used a lantern to light up his walk on the way home from his store each evening.

An undated photo showing Will at his desk inside his men's store
UNLV Libraries, Special Collections

Ed Von Tobel and his wife Mary on the left with Jake and Will Beckley on the right are seen watching flowing water from an artesian well on Ed and Jake's ranch in this 1909 photo
UNLV Libraries, Special Collections

Leva and Will Beckley visiting Indian springs in this circa 1915 photo
UNLV Libraries, Special Collections

A 1915 photo of Alta and Jake Beckley
on a road trip in Sierra Vista, Arizona
UNLV Libraries, Special Collections

During the summer of 1913 brother Jake bought lots on 4th Street near Fremont for a house. On August 27th he married Leva's younger sister Alta in Indiana where she was a teacher.

Will's store signage is seen on the left in this photo circa 1918. Will in the early days went by his initials U.W.
Courtesy of the Nevada State Museum, Las Vegas

In late June of 1913 there was a late-night fire in Will's store that resulted in a $9000 loss of goods and fixtures. The fire spread and caused $500 worth of damage to the adjoining Hotel Nevada. It was believed that someone left on a large electric ironing press. The local volunteer fire fighters took some 20 minutes to arrive. Using two streams of water it took them 20 minutes to extinguish the blaze. Will moved salvageable stock across Fremont Street into a temporary store. He collected $5000 in insurance monies. Repairs to the hotel were done and Will ordered new merchandise from Los Angeles as well as from the East coast. He reopened on August 23, 1913.

Photo circa 1920 of the Beckley Building
UNLV Libraries, Special Collections

One of Will's biggest competitors was M.C. Thomas who ran the large Thomas' Department Store just a short distance away at the southwest corner of Fremont and 1st Streets. In October of 1913 a fire seriously damaged the building it was housed in. After repairs were done, Thomas decided not to return. He rented his rebuilt corner store to Will for $112.50 per month. Will promised to operate an attractive store and opened "Beckley's Men's Furnishing Store" on November 10th. In 1914 Will was able to negotiate the purchase of the two-story cement block building from Thomas for $12,500. Upstairs used to be home for the town's original Opera House but now offered space to the American Legion and a variety of fraternal organizations. Will's new store had its official grand opening on November 26, 1914, which featured a ball and orchestra. It then became known as the Beckley Building.

During the summer of 1914 Will and Leva returned to Illinois to visit family and also traveled to Chicago, St. Paul, Winnipeg, Seattle, Portland, San Francisco and Los Angeles. They were gone for some 30 days.

Jake and Ed Von Tobel used their lumberyard earnings to finance alternating trips back to Fairbury, Illinois to visit their families. In late August of 1914 a large fire destroyed their lumberyard while Ed was away in Fairbury. It was a late-night fire that caused between $12,000 and $15,000 in damage. Insurance paid out just $4,500. Ed wanted to rebuild but Jake had enough of the lumber business. Ed used some of his share of the insurance money to buy out Jake.

An undated photo showing the large inventory of shoes stocked in Beckley's Men's Store
UNLV Libraries, Special Collections

Jake used his newly acquired money to build a home for Alta and himself on 3rd Street near Bridger. He also purchased a new Ford. Jake then went to work temporarily for brother Will at the clothing store.

In March of 1915, mother Magdalena passed away at age 73 while residing with son John in Illinois. A few weeks later, a son, Bruce, was born to Leva and Will. Doing well in his business, Will purchased two cottages in July on 4th Street between Fremont and Ogden. He paid $1000 and found renters.

Will Beckley holding his son Bruce is in the center of this 1916 photo taken inside his store
UNLV Libraries, Special Collections

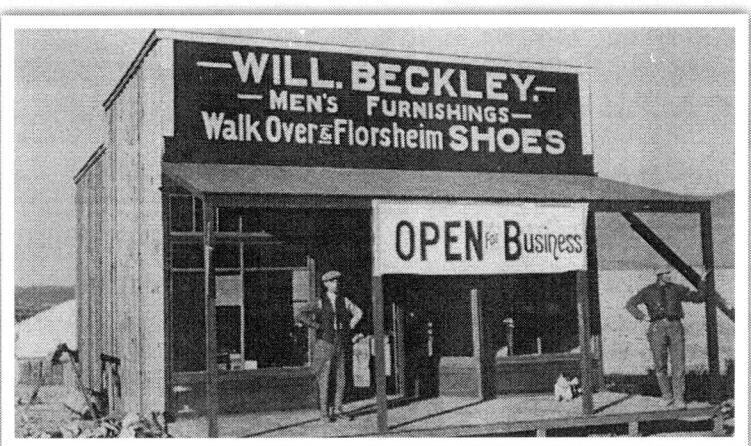

Photo circa early 1918 of Will's branch store in Goodsprings
UNLV Libraries, Special Collections

In 1917, with World War I underway, there was a great need for metals. Will decided to open a branch store in Goodsprings after noticing how many men were attracted there to work in the local mines.

Jake, with partners, had landed in April, 1916 a $900 city contract to drill a 600 foot deep well. When it was completed Ed and Jake leased out their Paradise Valley ranch. Jake then moved to Goodsprings to run Will's new branch store. It only remained in business for a year or so. When mining in the area declined after the war, Will decided to close it.

The Beckley clan poses for a photo in front of their upgraded clothing store in Goodsprings
UNLV Libraries, Special Collections

The Beckley's pose along the side of their Goodsprings store in 1918. From the left are Jake, a Mrs. Fayle, Will, a Mrs. Pemrose, Alta, little Bruce being held by grandpa Fred Grimes, and Leva.
UNLV Libraries, Special Collections

In August of 1916, Jake's leased ranch house in Paradise Valley along with established crops suffered severe damage after a big storm.

The year 1917 began with the birth of Will and Leva's daughter Virginia on January 26; their second and final child. Bruce now had a little sister. Will made numerous investments during 1917. He bought four lots from W.E. Hawkins for $500 at the southeast corner of Fremont and 6th Streets. He then paid $6,500 for a building on Fremont between 1st and 2nd Streets followed by another $6,500 for most of the empty lots on South 7th St. across from the site of the town's high school.

Jake rebuilt the ranch house. It was placed on stilts as seen in this circa 1917 photo.
UNLV Libraries, Special Collections

A 1917 photo of Bruce and Virginia Beckley.
Courtesy of the Nevada State Museum, Las Vegas

Jake and Alta had a child, Eunice, on November 27, 1917. She would be their only child.

Seen in this circa 1921 beach photo are Eunice on the left and her cousins Bruce and Virginia on the far right
Courtesy of the Nevada State Museum, Las Vegas

After the closure of the Goodsprings store, Will decided to try another branch store. This one was in Blythe, California and Jake would be his partner. It was about 200 miles away from Las Vegas and was operated by brother Jake. (It closed about five years later.)

While running the store in Blythe, Jake noticed how well cotton was growing in the area. Will and Jake partnered in buying 100 pounds of cottonseed and advertised their seed for sale, claiming growers could generate between $200 and $300 per acre harvested.

People pose in front of a Beckley road sign in this photo taken circa 1920. The sign lists both the Las Vegas and Blythe locations
UNLV Libraries, Special Collections

Photo circa 1920 of the Beckley & Beckley store in a Blythe, California hotel
UNLV Libraries, Special Collections

Locals came out to see the first plane to land in Las Vegas. Jake Beckley in seen in the center of this May 7, 1920, photo.
UNLV Libraries, Special Collections

Jake made friends with noted WWI pilot Randall Henderson in California. On May 7, 1920, Jake accompanied Randall from Blythe in a Curtiss-Jenny bi-plane as it became the first flight to ever land in Las Vegas. Residents were most excited.

In January of 1922 Will and four partners organized the Bank of Southern Nevada. It was housed in the Hotel Nevada. (The bank would close the last day of 1933.)

A circa 1923 photo of Leva, Virginia, Bruce and Will Beckley.
UNLV Libraries, Special Collections

Jake returned to live in Las Vegas during the summer of 1923 after they closed the Blythe store. Jake was now closer to oversee his ranch.

On July 23, 1923, the side wall (along 1st Street) of Will's men's store collapsed. As repairs were done, Will decided to add a back room dedicated to the sale of shoes. He was a major distributor of Florsheim Shoes. In November Jake moved into a home on 3rd Street and went to work for Will in his store.

February of 1924 saw Will do a store remodel. He created impressive 18 feet deep window display areas along with glass display cases in the lobby and lighting attached to the ceiling. That summer Will bought a new Buick.

 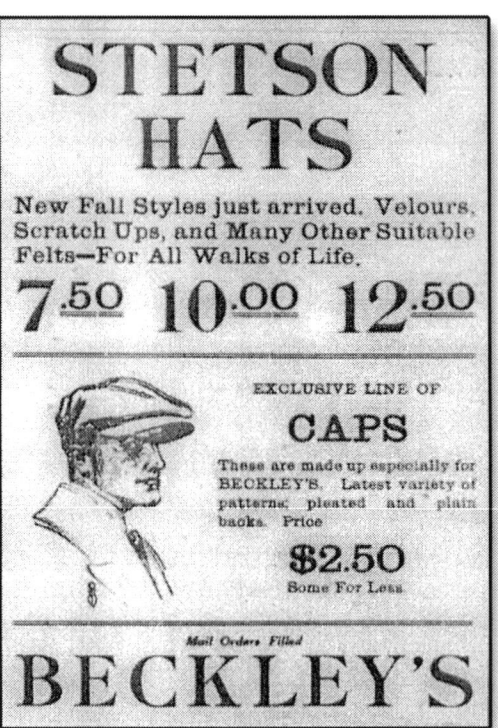 

Will was a regular advertiser in the Las Vegas Age newspaper. This ad is from September 9, 1922

A November 4, 1922, Las Vegas Age ad

A later ad in the July 24, 1926, Las Vegas Age

In January of 1925 the new Las Vegas Businessmen's Association was formed with Will as its treasurer. In April Will added on rooms to his home.

In June of 1927, Leva and Alta's father Fred Grimes became very ill in Wolcott, Indiana. He would pass in early July. That year Jake would sell his ranch for $1800 (today it would be worth many millions of dollars).

A photo circa 1931 of the now 3-story Beckley Building on the southwest corner of Fremont and 1st Street.
UNLV Libraries, Special Collections; Beckley Photo Collection (0148 0016)]

In early 1929 Will borrowed $20,000 to add a third floor to his building. Work began in April on what was to become the first 3-story building in Las Vegas. The east wall was replaced, and windows were added. The inside underwent a remodeling project. The store remained open during all of this work. An arcade was added along 1st Street, south of Fremont, and the new top floor would offer 20 office spaces for lease. An almost thirteen foot long red and green neon sign was attached to the building and remained there until the early 1940's. A formal grand opening was held in December of 1929.

Photo circa 1931 of the front entrance to Beckley's store on Fremont.
Courtesy of the Clark County Museum

A photo from 1930. Jake is seen on the far left and Will on the right.
*UNLV Libraries, Special Collections;
Beckley Photo Collection (0148 0013)*

Beckley ad in the January 29, 1932, Las Vegas Age

In mid-August of 1931 Jake started building a new home at 4th and Gass. Gambling was legalized in Nevada that year and casinos began appearing on Fremont. They brought added business to Will's store. In late 1931 Will took charge of the local relief committee. The Great Depression was underway, and the Red Cross was expected to come to Las Vegas to assist. A year later, in November of 1932 Emma Grimes, mother of Leva and Alta, would pass away at age 78.

In 1939 Jake built and operated the Acre Auto Court at 1031 So. 5th Street. That year, Will and Leva's daughter Virginia was married. In October Will joined Ed Von Tobel on a trip to Fairbury and then went on to the World's Fair in New York City.

In June of 1940 Jake was hospitalized in Los Angeles, awaiting surgery. After his operation he was able to return to Las Vegas a few weeks later. In August his daughter Eunice married David Boles of Salt Lake City. In September Jake fell ill again from a recurring stomach ailment. He passed away at home from cancer at age 65 on October 6. Jake loved to fish and hunt. He was buried in Woodlawn Cemetery.

Photo of Alta Beckley in the 1930's
*UNLV Libraries, Special Collections;
Dokter Photo Collection (0012 0085)*

In September 1941 Will discussed leasing the ground floor store of his building with Will Scherer who wanted to open a casino. Scherer obtained his gambling license from the Chief of Police in October and Will would close his store in January of 1942; he maintained in retirement an office on the second floor of the building. He had been in the clothing business for some 34 years since arriving in Las Vegas.

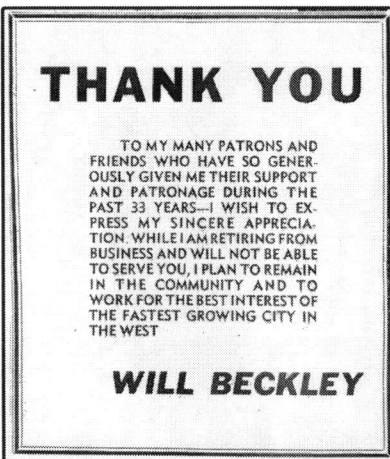

Will ran a farewell ad in the January 12, 1942, issue of the Las Vegas Review Journal

January 13, 1942, Las Vegas Review Journal ad by Will to liquidate store fixtures

Scherer would open his Pioneer Club in the Beckley Building after Will sold off its contents. Will retained ownership of the building and kept his name sign atop of it. There was a housing shortage in Las Vegas in 1941. Will owned land south of Charleston and was approved to open a housing tract on the property. He focused his attention on lot sales along with his many other real estate interests.

In April of 1950 Will purchased Walter Bracken's home at 714 So. 7th Street for $18,000 and lived out his life there.

Undated photo of the Pioneer Club which replaced Will's men's store
UNLV Libraries, Special Collections;
Sherwin Scoop Garside Photo Collection (0067 0037)

Jake's widow Alta, while residing at 517 Park Paseo near her auto court, suffered a stroke in March of 1951. She was hospitalized six weeks with paralysis. She passed in early May at age 60 and was buried next to Jake in Woodlawn. Daughter Eunice and husband David Boles inherited the Acre Auto Court. They had two children.

Will was ill most of 1964. In January of 1965 he was in critical condition for weeks. He died at home at the end of the month. He was buried at the Palm Desert Memorial Mausoleum. Will left behind his children Bruce and Virginia, four grandchildren and one great-grand child.

The year prior to his death, Will was pleased to learn that the school district would be naming a planned elementary school after him. The Beckley Elementary School was built and had a dedication ceremony in November of 1966. Family members made a nice donation to help the school's library get established.

As the years passed, most of the quaint old cottages and homes in the downtown Las Vegas area had disappeared to make way for new commercial buildings, including casinos. The Beckley's 1912 California-style cottage

Eunice Lois Beckley in her 1939 UNR graduation photo
Ancestry.org

An April 12, 1964, photo of Will Beckley at a Rotary Club meeting
Courtesy of the Clark County Museum

at 120 So. 4th Street (between Fremont and Carson and now part of the D Hotel) was possibly the last one remaining and Leva in 1978 at age 93 was still residing there. With her health failing, Leva would move in with her daughter and the family worked with the Las Vegas Junior League to donate the home and have it moved to the Southern Nevada Museum in Henderson (now the Clark County Museum) which had plans to establish their Heritage Street of preserved historic buildings. The furniture was placed in storage and before the house was moved it played host in February 1979 to a farewell party. The Beckley House became the first building placed on Heritage Street which opened in 1983. 120 So. 4th Street became a parking lot rented to the city by Bruce and Virginia Beckley.

The Beckley house after arriving at the museum
Courtesy of the Clark County Museum

The Beckley house as it sits today on Heritage Street at the Clark County Museum
Courtesy of the Clark County Museum

With her health continuing to decline for many weeks, Leva went to a local residential hotel. She passed away at age 93 in June of 1979. She was remembered as a 1911 charter member of the Mesquite Club. She was also a charter member of the city's first bridge club.

A photo of Leva Beckley that was published in a brochure by the Frontier Fidelity Savings and Loan Association

Circa 1965 photo of Bruce Beckley
UNLV Libraries, Special Collections; Ferron-Bracken Photo Collection (0001 0095)

Photo from the early 2000's of Virginia Beckley

Son Bruce Beckley was born in the Beckley House. He went on to study law at Stanford University. During World War II he worked for the Navy at U.C. Berkley doing underground sound research. After the war he taught law at the San Francisco Law School. In 1954 he went into private practice in Las Vegas. In 1967 he started a law firm that specialized in patent, probate, and real estate law. He would serve as President of the Las Vegas Chamber of Commerce and was on the board of directors of numerous companies. He married and had two sons, Bob and Doug. He died on October 6, 1986, at the Nathan Adelson Hospice at age 71.

Daughter Virginia was also born in the Beckley House. She graduated Las Vegas High School at age 16. She attended Scripps College in California followed by the University of Nevada Reno where she met her husband Jack Richardson (they were married in 1939). Jack managed Will's clothing store until he was activated as a military pilot in August of 1941. Virginia and Jack had two sons, Robert and William. After the war they started numerous businesses -- The Las Vegas Surplus Store, Rich's Hardware & Men's Clothing, and the Gold Strike Inn and Casino in Boulder City. Virginia passed away in August of 2017 at age 100.

Jake's sole child Eunice had become a teacher. She died in 1984 at age 66.

Jake and Will Beckley contributed to the growth of Las Vegas. Will became a noted clothing merchant with Jake involved in the lumber business and ranching, eventually going to work in Will's stores. Will outlived his brother by some 24 years. Their children went on to also serve the Las Vegas community. Before his death, Will recalled his two greatest business deal regrets. In the early 1930's he passed on buying for $15,000 the northeast corner of Fremont and 2nd from wealthy Nevada banker George Winfield. The corner would eventually become home to the Fremont Hotel and Casino. He also passed on buying 80 lots along 6th and 7th Streets near Bridger for just $3,000.

Unlike other early pioneers, the Beckley brothers had little interest in local politics or mining. They pursued what made them happy. They both had interesting and productive lives.

Chapter 11
Walter Bracken
Postmaster and Railroad Agent

Most American historians are in agreement that many major western cities would never have developed without the expansion of railroad lines and the opportunities for growth they brought with them. Las Vegas can definitely be placed on that list. Once the tracks were laid, Las Vegas was connected to many markets in other states. The railroad company's executives would situate key employees in the Las Vegas valley to manage their affairs. Those people would play key roles in the growth of Southern Nevada. The most prominent and influential agent in Las Vegas for the railroad was Walter Bracken. For over four decades he played a huge role in the growth and development of the city.

Walter R. Bracken was born in 1870 in Mount Pleasant, Ohio. He earned a degree in civil engineering in Pennsylvania. In 1901 Walter was selected to be part of a survey team sent from Utah into Southern Nevada via buckboard to search for a feasible train route and sources of water. Wealthy and influential Montana Senator William A. Clark was seeking to connect Salt Lake City to Southern California by rail and had competition from E.W. Harriman of the Union Pacific Railroad. They would eventually merge their efforts.

Senator William Clark arrived in Las Vegas with his young wife on his personal train on April 22, 1906
UNLV Libraries, Special Collections

Undated photo of James Ross Clark

In 1901 Clark had incorporated the San Pedro, Los Angeles, Salt Lake Railroad. Early survey teams had already identified an abundance of water in the Las Vegas valley area. The railroad negotiated the purchase of Kiel Ranch in 1901 followed by the Stewart Ranch in 1902. Both ranches had flowing creeks and could make excellent sites for a possible train depot along with facilities where railway equipment could be serviced. The Senator placed his younger brother, J. Ross Clark of Los Angeles, in charge of his railroad with the title of Vice-President. J. Ross Clark began making decisions about both ranches. In 1903 he assigned his second cousin, Dr. J.K.W. Bracken (Walter's brother), to be in charge of the Stewart Ranch which included all its structures, crops, livestock and goods. Walter Bracken would later join his brother on the ranch to help out. The Bracken brothers accepted the fact that railroad executives wanted to micromanage the ranch. Every financial decision had to have the approval of the railroad, which was extremely penny conscious, to say the least.

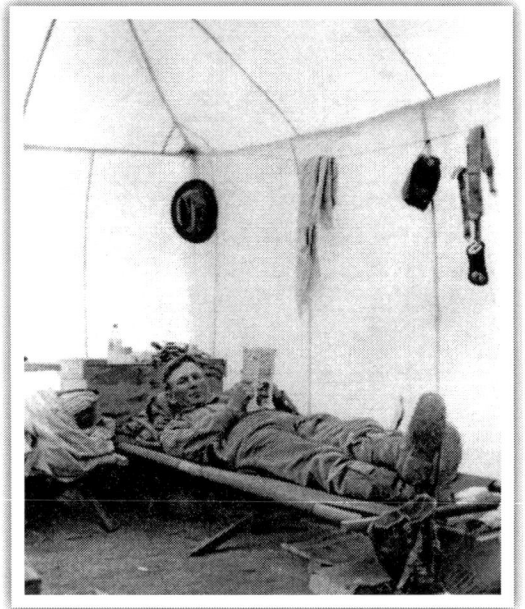

Walter Bracken resting in a tent in an undated photo
UNLV Libraries, Special Collections

Undated photo of the Las Vegas Land and Water Co. building on Main Street
UNLV Libraries, Special Collections

The railroad purchased numerous tents in Salt Lake City in October of 1904 for use on the old Stewart Ranch. Walter resided in one of them.

From 1903 into early 1905 work on the rail lines connecting southern California to Salt Lake City proceeded at at a rapid pace. As noted earlier, the Salt Lake to Las Vegas portion was completed in October of 1904 followed a few months later by the Los Angeles to Las Vegas stretch in January of 1905.

The railroad would establish a subsidiary, the Las Vegas Land and Water Co., to administer its proposed townsite and its vast land and water holdings. J. Ross Clark would be in charge acting from Los Angeles and Walter Bracken was appointed his local managing agent residing in the area. Walter clearly understood that he could not make any important decisions without first consulting with railroad executives.

Early 1905 photo of the wooden ranch general store that was moved to Main Street
UNLV Libraries, Special Collections

Even though the railroad desired the water rights of the ranch, they did not like taking on the responsibility of maintaining it. So they made the decision to begin leasing it. Dr. Bracken would move on. In 1893 Helen Stewart had established the first post office in the area on her ranch. Walter took over her duties of running the small post office and became its postmaster. He received no compensation, but being postmaster was considered a position of honor.

On March 1, 1905, Walter Bracken signed a $1000 (up front) one year lease to occupy and make use of the ranch. He was granted future renewals of the lease. Walter, along with a partner, was able to buy the hay, grain, lumber and meat shops on the ranch for $2800. They formed the Las Vegas Mercantile Company.

May 15, 1905, was day one of the two-day land auction conducted by the railroad to sell lots laid out in blocks in the townsite they had just recently completed surveying. The very first passenger train from Los Angeles arrived in Las Vegas that morning transporting many enthusiastic prospective buyers. C.C. Whitemore, the railroad's attorney, was in charge of the auction which saw 176 choice lots of the 1200 up for sale purchased by eager bidders. Walter was a successful bidder of one lot.

Undated photo of newlyweds Anna and Walter Bracken
UNLV Libraries, Special Collections

Anna Bracken on the front porch of their adobe home on the ranch
UNLV Libraries, Special Collections

Just days after the auction, Walter would marry Anna Johnson (a University of Nevada, Reno graduate) in Salt Lake City. Anna hailed from Eureka, Nevada and was the school principal in the town of Delamar. The newlyweds would return to live in Las Vegas after honeymooning in San Francisco and Los Angeles. They were honored with a grand celebration on the ranch.

June 1905 photo of the post office on the west side of Main Street near Fremont
UNLV Libraries, Special Collections

The post office can be seen in this 1905 photo to the right of Kuhn's store which temporarily housed the First State Bank
UNLV Libraries, Special Collections

Bracken recognized that his post office on the ranch needed to be closer to the new upcoming town where people would build homes and businesses would be established. In early 1905 it was relocated to the west side of Main Street just south of Fremont Street, adjacent to land where a depot would be be built. Soon thereafter, the general store from the ranch would be moved next to the post office and sold to Norman Kuhn for his mercantile company. When the railroad needed the land for their depot project, Kuhn's store and the post office were asked to move. Kuhn moved his store directly across to the other side of Main Street. The post office tent was relocated to the north side of Fremont Street near 1st Street, adjacent to a wooden two-story structure built to temporarily house the First State Bank.

Believing a railroad would soon be built from Las Vegas to Beatty to serve mining operations, Bracken invested with a partner in a ranch in Indian Springs, some 45 miles outside of Las Vegas. He was pretty sure the area would become a future railroad stop as it had a healthy supply of runoff water from Mt. Charleston. For some unknown reason they wound up putting the ranch up for auction and as expected the railroad swooped in to buy it. They kept Walter on for a short while to manage the ranch while they drew up plans for a railroad stop that would include lodging, food, and a general merchandise store. (A line was built and train service between Las Vegas and Indian Springs commenced in 1907.)

In 1905 Bracken had become the president of two local companies -- The Home Building and Loan Association and the Vegas Artesian Water Syndicate. Both began with $100,000 stock offerings. Walter would supervise the installation of the town's first water system which consisted of hollowed out redwood logs tied together by metal hoops (a method cheaper than using iron pipes which pleased the thrifty railroad executives; it remained in use until 1931). Also in 1905, Bracken was involved with the Las Vegas Mercantile Co. on the ranch; it supplied fresh meat to the town. In 1906 Walter was fully in charge of the railroad's powerful Las Vegas Land and Water Company. Walter also began serving on the town's newly created volunteer fire department. He was the young town's busiest resident.

The post office was directly behind the windows on the right of the First State Bank
UNLV Libraries, Special Collections

Walter Bracken at his post office desk in May of 1908
UNLV Libraries, Special Collections

Anna Bracken inside the post office in a 1908 photo. She often assisted Walter in the post office
UNLV Libraries, Special Collections

In January of 1906 Bracken was able to move his post office operation into the beautiful newly completed brick building housing the First State Bank on the northeast corner of Fremont and 1st. It occupied the front portion of the building facing Fremont. Bracken advertised in the local Age newspaper that he was a notary and word also went out that water bills were now payable to him inside the bank.

Walter and his wife Anna were very socially active in numerous clubs and civic organizations. They hosted many a dinner at the ranch and Walter was a charter member of both the Rotary Club (launched in his house) and the Masons. He would serve as the treasurer of the Elks and when a Chamber of Commerce was formed he became a very active member. Walter was also a very spirited participant in the local Republican Party. Anna helped establish the city's library system.

When the Brackens renewed their ranch lease in 1906, the railroad insisted he use no part of it for public purposes. They also requested that he do a general clean-up and repair adobe structures on the property. In November of 1906 Walter sold his interest in the Las Vegas Mercantile Co. but retained its hay and grain operations. There was a serious 250-acre fire on the ranch in September of 1907. It was started by a trespasser and Walter had to request assistance from the local town to put it out. The Brackens would exit the ranch in 1908 and purchase an existing house at 410 Fremont Street which they would call home for the next 37 years.

Photo circa 1908 of the Bracken residence
UNLV Libraries, Special Collections

Walter Bracken at home in this undated photo. The Brackens had a large collection of Indian baskets and rugs throughout their house.
UNLV Libraries, Special Collections

In December of 1908 Walter became vice-president of the First State Bank, a position that he kept until the bank was sold decades later. In April of 1909 Walter attended the State's Republican Convention in Winnemucca. He was a very busy gentleman.

Photo circa 1912 of the new site of the post office in the Griffith Building on the southwest corner of Fremont and 2nd Streets. The popular Majestic Theater opened in space on the second floor.
UNLV Libraries, Special Collections

By early 1912, with the town growing, Bracken had to start searching for a new larger space for his post office. He settled on a spot at the southwest corner of Fremont and 2nd in the recently finished E.W. Griffith building. When the Democrats gained influence in the area in 1914, Bracken decided to resign as postmaster believing they would not want a Republican in the position. In April of 1915 Walter's father, J.P. Bracken, passed away in Pasadena, California. The Brackens were a very close family with the brothers and sister Edith often visiting each other and their parents for birthdays, holidays, and anniversaries. None of the three siblings ever had any children.

Photo of Bracken circa 1915
UNLV Libraries, Special Collections

Well into the 1920's and beyond, Bracken continued his duties as the agent and voice of the Union Pacific Railroad which had purchased the San Pedro - Las Vegas - Salt Lake Railroad. Walter continued to seek the approval of railroad executives prior to making any important decisions. He would take many business trips over the years to large and small cities in Utah, Nevada, and California. He was a workaholic and didn't really like to take time away from his responsibilities. He did occasionally vacation in California and Washington State, but not that often. In 1925 the Brackens found themselves in Santa Barbara when a large earthquake struck. Twelve people were killed and hundreds injured. Luckily the Brackens escaped unhurt. Even their car did not get a scratch when their hotel garage suffered serious damage. His wife Anna would often travel on her own to the east coast as well as to Canada, Asia and Europe.

Undated photo of Walter Bracken, circa 1930's
Courtesy of the Nevada State Museum, Las Vegas

1940's photo of Walter and Anna Bracken
UNLV Libraries, Special Collections;
Glenn Davis Photo Collection (0020 0249)

In 1931 Walter was appointed a member of the newly created Nevada State Board of Education. By the 1940's Walter's eyesight began to deteriorate. After 45 years of continuous service to the town and the railroad, Bracken was forced to retire and also resigned from the Board of Education. They had moved in 1945 to 714 So. 7th Street. He and Anna would then spend their summers in San Francisco.

On January 2, 1950, Anna would fall ill and die at the age of 65 from a heart attack. Anna and Walter were married almost 45 years. In April of that year Walter sold his home on So. 7th Street to Las Vegas pioneers Mr. and Mrs. Will Beckley for $1800. Unfortunately Walter died a few months later on July 13. Walter was blind his last year of life. At the time of his passing, Walter had the distinction of being Las Vegas' longest continuous resident. He once admitted to being a "grubstaker" over the years, only to admit that he never made any real profits. He did own many parcels of land inside and outside of the city limits.

Walter Bracken will be remembered as an early postmaster of Las Vegas and for his role in making many land, water, and railroad related decisions that helped the young town of Las Vegas grow and develop into an important thriving desert community. He was a most notable early Las Vegas pioneer. Walter and Anna Bracken are buried in Woodlawn Cemetery.

Chapter 12
Moyd C. Thomas, Sr.
Grocer

Las Vegas had numerous early merchants who quickly set up temporary stores right after the railroad's land auction of town lots in mid-May of 1905. One of them was Moyd Charles Thomas who began selling general supplies and food staples out of a wooden shack on 2nd Street, south of Fremont.

Moyd's father, Charles Caleb Thomas, was born in 1828 in London, England and immigrated as a youth to the United States in 1835. His mother, Nancy Edds Moffatt, was born in Virginia about 1830. The two resided in Peoria, Illinois where they had three children. Their first born was son Felix in July of 1856. Harry L. Thomas came next in 1859. Moyd, born in 1862, was Nancy and Charles' final child.

In 1869 Caleb moved the family to the Oakland, California area. They arrived on just the second passenger train ever to run on the Union & Central Pacific railway line. It took eleven days to travel from Peoria to California. They would call Eureka, California home. In many early official documents, Moyd would appear under his given name of Moysey. In the early 1880's Moyd would go off on his own. On August 12, 1883, he married Christena Hutz in San Diego, California. She was 18 and he was 21. They would live in Winchester, California and have three children in the 1880's. In 1891 the family was living in Ukiah, California.

Nothing is known about Moyd from the early 1890's until he shows up as a guest in Ladd's tent hotel in Las Vegas in March of 1905. In July of 1905 he was already operating his grocery store on South 2nd Street and soon thereafter moved it to 1st Street, south of Fremont. Moyd moved his business yet again in early 1906 to a new building on the north side of Fremont just east of the First State Bank. In May of 1907 he purchased a horse and cart so he could make deliveries.

Undated photo of M.C. Thomas.
UNLV Libraries, Special Collections

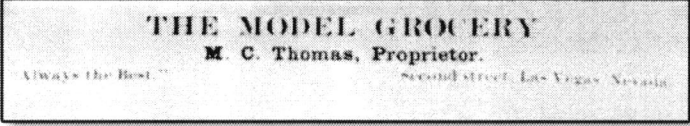

February 24, 1906, Las Vegas Age ad.
Thomas called his early store The Model Grocery

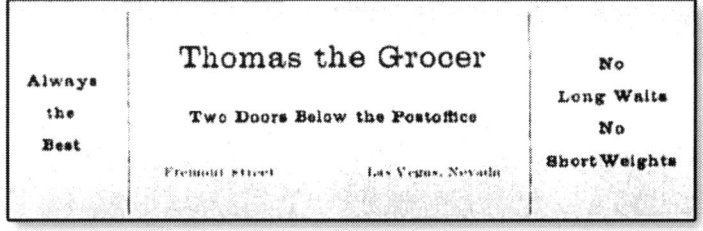

June 9, 1906, Las Vegas Age ad. When he moved his store to the north side of Fremont Street, he began calling his business "Thomas the Grocer"

Late in 1907 the local bank which owned the the southwest corner of Fremont and 1st Street began building a large two-story cement block building. It would be known as the Masonic Temple Building and the top floor would be home to the town's Opera House. Moyd made arrangements to rent the large downstairs space for his Thomas' Department Store. He moved in February of 1908 and began selling mostly groceries and some general staples and clothing. A week later the opera house upstairs opened with $1 tickets sold across the street at the Wilson Pharmacy.

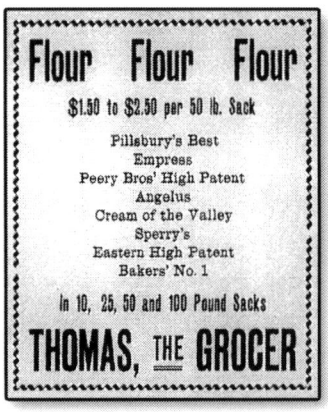

July 25, 1907, Las Vegas Age ad

Undated photo showing a typical but unidentified early Las Vegas grocery store interior
UNLV Libraries, special Collections

Photo circa 1908 of the newly completed building at the southwest corner of Fremont and 1st Streets
UNLV Libraries, Special Collections

Undated photo of Thomas' Department Store at the southwest corner of Fremont and 1st Streets
UNLV Libraries, Special Collections

Photo circa 1912 of the Thomas Department Store with its signage up
UNLV Libraries, Special Collections

In December of 1908, Moyd's nephew Will arrived from Riverside, California to work in the grocery store. He resided with the family. Just before Christmas Moyd had a serious accident. His horsed slipped while rounding a corner at Fremont and 2nd Street. The horse fell and threw Moyd to the ground. The horse rolled over Moyd leaving him bruised and unconscious. Luckily, he would mend, having to nurse a knee injury for a few months.

In early 1909 Moyd had a house built on 1st Street for the family. He was able to walk to work. That June he attended a large exposition in Seattle. As the months went by, Moyd became more involved in civic activities; he joined the Masons and became an Elk. In May of 1910 he convinced other local merchants to help fund a band composed of local residents to perform once a week on Fremont Street. He believed the lively music would attract customers to his store. In July of 1910 all of the town's grocers agreed to close their stores on Sundays. That same month Moyd joined the Town Board of Trustees. In August Moyd made a large purchase of goods for $11,000 to restock his large store. He became a regular advertiser in the local Las Vegas Age newspaper.

July 4, 1908
Las Vegas Age ad

February 13, 1909
Las Vegas Age ad

March 13, 1909
Las Vegas Age ad

May 15, 1909
Las Vegas Age ad

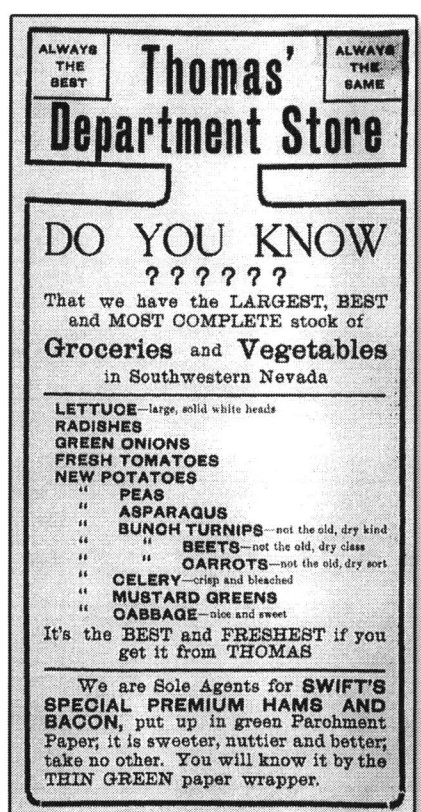

April 16, 1910
Las Vegas Age ad

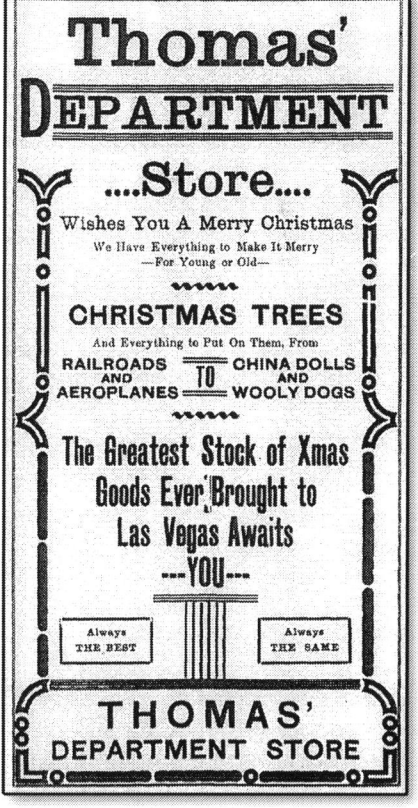

December 15, 1910
Las Vegas Age ad

The Thomas' Department Store was most successful, having a prominent corner location in the business area of the still young town. Moyd had saved the funds to buy the entire building his store was in for $17,500 from the First State Bank in December of 1910. The building had 40 feet of frontage on Fremont Street and was 105 feet deep along 1st Street. A few months later the Opera House would move one block east and become the Majestic Theater. The upper floor was rented for offices and lodge meeting space. Moyd's parents, Caleb and Nancy, made a visit in January of 1911 to Las Vegas to see their son's building and store. It was their first trip outside of California since arriving there some 41 years earlier. Later that year they decided to move to Las Vegas to live out their remaining years.

Moyd served on the Commerce Committee of the town's Chamber of Commerce. When Las Vegas became a city in the summer of 1911, he ran unsuccessfully for a seat on the Board of Commissioners.

In June of 1911 Moyd conducted a big store sale, letting it be known that he would pay the train fair of any customer who spent over $25 if they lived over 30 miles away from town. That summer Moyd tried to make a deal with local postmaster Walter Bracken to move the post office from the First State Bank across the street into his department store. He was offering 1000 square feet. The deal collapsed when neither party was willing to cover the cost of needed remodeling.

Las Vegas' Greatest Sale
THOMAS' DEPARTMENT STORE

EVERY ARTICLE AND ITEM IN THE STORE A REAL BARGAIN
THE NEXT 14 DAYS

$18,000   WORTH $18,000

In offering this sale to the public, we announce that all arrangements have been made, for reducing the goods, employing extra help, and preparing the stock for quick inspection. Everything is in complete readiness, and a sale that is different, a real bonafide, grand and collossal merchandising battle which is without counterpart or parallel in the history of modern merchandising. There will positively be no exaggerations made and there cannot and will not be any dissatisfaction. We are giving the biggest sale in the history of Las Vegas. A sale inaugurated along intelligent lines, and where every dollar's worth of merchandise will be right before your eyes and marked plainly. People will buy as they never bought before.

It is a public sale with real genuine bargains, and an original direct appeal to every thinking man, woman and child for miles around. We want you to come and see that we have carefully prepared for this sale. We offer a broad legitimate guarantee that upon demand we will exchange, give back or refund any dollar paid us for any article during the entire sale that is not satisfactory. The goods are marked right. The reductions are plain and simple, the character of the goods by far the best. The selection is well made.   Our conditions necessitate a sale.   Stock was closed down.

Date is Final!   The Place You Know!   A Sale You Cant Forget!

Ladies' and Childrens' Shoes and Oxfords at almost one-half price.

June 17, 1911, Las Vegas Age ad

In April of 1912 Moyd served on a committee of businessmen calling for the establishment of an organized and paid fire department. He was a major proponent of improved fire protection. The town still had a poorly organized volunteer fire department. In May the volunteers all resigned as they felt they had little support from town leaders.

Ironically, a few weeks later on May 19, 1912, a large 3 a.m. fire destroyed Thomas' Department Store. It was the biggest fire in Las Vegas since the Overland Hotel a block away burned down a year earlier. Moyd suffered a $60,000 loss in merchandise, fixtures and the structure itself. He was able to recover $36,000 in insurance money. He vowed that with the help of his two sons, Moyd Jr. and Roy, he would rebuild a structure of reinforced concrete on the same spot.

1912 photo taken shortly after the fire at the northwest corner of Fremont and 1st Streets
UNLV Libraries, Special Collections

Another photo of the fire damage to Moyd's building
UNLV Libraries, Special Collections

There was a lot of debris to be cleared away so it would take many months to rebuild. Therefore, in July of 1912 Moyd purchased the Boggs Brothers Grocery store (a nearby competitor) to use as a temporary store. In October Moyd's new structure was under construction. He successfully petitioned the town to maintain a fire hose in a stand behind his new building. The new store opened on November 11, 1912. He made his two sons partners and installed a freight elevator from the basement to the main floor.

Sadly, in August of 1913 there was another early morning fire in his store which resulted this time in losses of $13,000. Insurance only paid off $5000. To make matters worse, Moyd's wife Christena filed for divorce in October. Moyd, along with the help of his two sons, again moved into the Bogg's Building across the street just west of the corner pharmacy. Moyd was becoming discouraged by the repeated fires. When his building was repaired a few months after the fire, he sold it to Will Beckley, a very prominent merchant of men's furnishings. Moyd's brother Harry and his two sons Will and Arthur would buy a major interest in the grocery business in

August 30, 1913, Las Vegas Age announcement

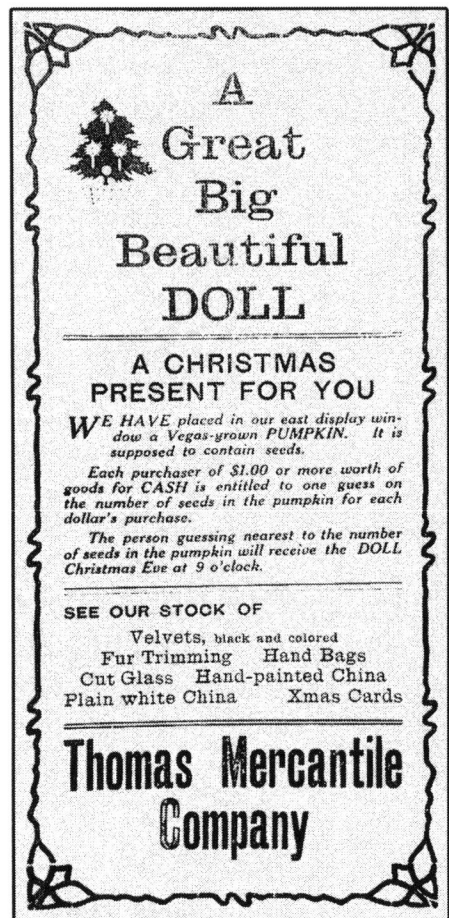

December 1913 Las Vegas Age ad placed by Harry Thomas

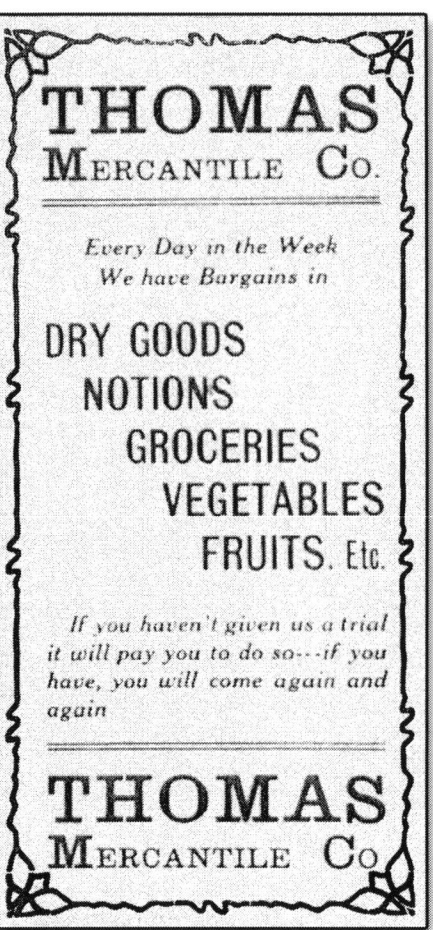

Thomas Mercantile Co. ad in the April 25, 1914, Las Vegas Age

November. Harry did well in the Boggs Building, even paying for expanding the building 40 feet to the rear. He added more general merchandise items to his inventory and renamed the business the "Thomas Mercantile Company". Moyd retained the title of President but went into retirement.

In late January of 1914 father Caleb Thomas passed away at age 86. He was buried in Woodlawn Cemetery. Four months later there was a fire in Harry's store that did some $5000 damage to his stock and the Boggs building. In June repairs started and Harry conducted a damaged goods fire sale. The business would resume operation.

Sometime after his divorce in 1913, Moyd remarried again. He and his wife Lina moved into a new house on 1st Street in November of 1914. Moyd's mother Nancy passed away on March 11, 1915, and was buried alongside her husband at Woodlawn Cemetery. In June Moyd's brother Harry sold the business and moved to Riverside, California for his wife's health.

In August of 1915 Moyd and Lina left on a long 2-month auto trip to expositions in San Diego and San Francisco. They visited Yosemite Valley and Lake Tahoe. Moyd fell ill during the trip and required hospitalization. He suffered a stomach hemorrhage and passed away on September 19, 1915, at age 53. Moyd was buried in the Hollywood Cemetery. Second wife Lina would return to live in Las Vegas for just an additional six months before moving away.

Moyd and first wife Christena did have three children in the 1880's -- Roy, Moyd Jr., and daughter Pearl. Roy was their first, born in May of 1884. He was followed by Moyd, Jr. in 1885 and Pearl in 1889.

After Moyd and his sons turned over their grocery store to Harry Thomas, Moyd Jr. and Roy left Las Vegas on a long journey to California and then Oregon looking for business opportunities. Roy would spend some time in Riverside, California before returning to live in Las Vegas in late 1915. In 1918 he registered for the WWI draft back in Riverside. In August he and brother Moyd Jr. would lease 2000 acres in Murietta, California to try their hands at growing wheat.

In the early 1920's Roy was a special deputy sheriff in California who was doing bootlegging on the side, providing liquor to people in Los Angeles. In 1925 he was arrested and fined $500. He also did a six-month jail sentence. He then returned to farming in Murietta. A short time later he was riding in a friend's car when they got into an argument that resulted in an exchange of blows. Roy suffered a severe head injury and died. With no witnesses, his friend was not prosecuted.

Moyd, Jr. married Bessie Mae Thompson a few years after he left Las Vegas. Bessie was born in Kansas in 1887. She was just a few years younger than her husband and bore him two sons, Moyd C. Thomas III in 1918 (Portland, Oregon) and Loren Bruce in 1920 (Corona, California). The family lived in Camarillo, California. They divorced in 1927 after Bessie accused Moyd Jr. of cheating. Bessie died in May of 1946 in Los Angeles. Moyd, Jr. went on to sell real estate in the 1930's in Beverly Hills, California and passed away on July 1, 1949, in Ventura, California.

Moyd Sr. and Christena Thomas' third child was daughter Pearl Irene Thomas. In July of 1914 she married Dee Petty of Los Angeles. She was 25 and he was 28. They had two boys -- Leonard in 1916 (Los Angeles) and Donald in 1919 (Nampa, Idaho). Pearl passed away young in 1927 and her husband in Las Vegas in 1963.

Moyd C. Thomas, Sr. was certainly not the most exciting or important early Las Vegas merchant. However, he was one of the pioneer grocers who cared for his community. He worked hard to supply goods to the residents of the young town.

Chapter 13
E.W. Griffith
Businessman, Contractor, Public Servant

It might be difficult to top the vast contributions of E.W. Griffith and his son Robert towards the growth of Las Vegas and the improved quality of life they bestowed upon residents.

Edmond William Griffith was born on September 9, 1862, in L'Avenir, Quebec, Canada. He attended Knowlton Academy, graduating in 1881. In March of 1882 he settled in Winnipeg, Canada and in 1883 contracted to build a bridge there. The next year he worked on a railroad grade. He was able to amass some $15,000 in savings which he used to buy property in Western Canada. He farmed and ranched his land until 1885 when he sold his holdings for $19,000 (a nice sum in those days). E.W. then headed to California in 1894 and resided in Pasadena where he lined up contract work related to road development with the city. He married 24-year-old Aura M. Beach on June 8, 1896 and became a naturalized citizen of the United States on October 22, 1898. Young son Robert, their only child, was born on January 12, 1899. Sadly, Aura would pass away young in March of 1904 when Robert was just five years old.

Undated photo circa 1910's of E.W. Griffith
UNLV Libraries, Special Collections

E.W. Griffith was hired in 1904 by wealthy Montana Senator William A. Clark and his railroad company to build a roundhouse for steam engine maintenance in the new town of Las Vegas. Once finished in early 1905, E.W. decided to take a chance by remaining in the new desert community. He attended the May 1905 railroad auction of town lots and wound up purchasing two on the southwest corner of Fremont and 2nd plus a lot on South 1st Street. He returned to California to retrieve his possessions and young son Robert to relocate to Las Vegas. They would live in a tent he constructed. E.W. would put his contractor skills to good use in the young town.

1905 photo of Clayson and Griffith's first store together
UNLV Libraries, Special Collections

In October of 1905 E.W. purchased a wooden and canvas tent-like structure on 1st Street. He partnered with Frank Clayson to open the town's first hardware store that sold saddles, saddlebags, wagon accessories, furniture, and mining supplies. Clayson had previously opened a furniture and household goods store on Wilson Ave. in McWilliams' townsite.

Photo circa 1909 of Griffith's partner Frank Clayson when he was Grandmaster of the Masonic Lodge
UNLV Libraries, Special Collections

E.W. would scour the surrounding desert for sickly burros which he brought back to health and sold at their general store.

Griffith was able to enroll in a Los Angeles course on embalming techniques which enabled him to become Las Vegas's first undertaker.

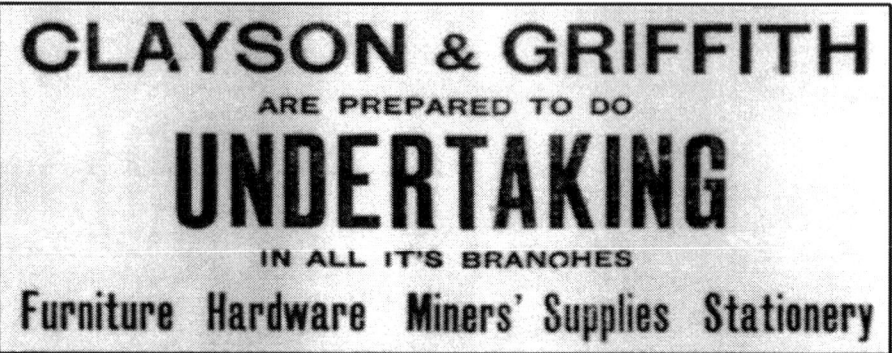

September 2, 1905, Las Vegas Times ad

In December of 1905 E.W. landed a contract to construct a large two-story brick building on the south side of Fremont as an annex to the nearly completed Hotel Nevada on the corner of Main Street. It was to be 100 feet wide and 65 feet deep and of the same height as the hotel to blend in. The first floor was for stores and J.F. Miller, owner of the hotel, would use the upper floor for additional lodging. The structure was completed in March of 1906.

As a leading citizen, E.W. joined the Las Vegas Artesian Water Syndicate in November of 1906. He was also directly involved with the construction of the first school and large church in Las Vegas.

E.W. Griffith worked with banker John S. Park and local judge W.R. Thomas to organize a Masonic Lodge in Las Vegas. He would faithfully serve the Masons in many capacities over his lifetime.

Griffith and Clayson had a store just to the right of the First State Bank in this undated photo
UNLV Libraries, Special Collections

In 1906 E.W. travelled to Mexico and returned with burros to sell locally. In 1907, he and Clayson formed the Nevada Oil and Fuel Company with E.W serving as president and manager. They sold gasoline, kerosene, oils, and distillate oil for heating and cooking purposes. In April of that year, they leased the Fred Fallas Building on Fremont to open another store, one dedicated to the sale of just home furnishing and carpeting. They also opened a third store directly adjacent to the new First State Bank on Fremont which specialized in hardware and mining supplies. Griffith and Clayson would sell that one to Mrs. Dan V. Noland in December who started the "Pioneer Furniture Store".

In early 1908 E.W. purchased three lots to the west of the ones he owned on the southwest corner of Fremont and 2nd. He had plans to build a nice structure on his five lots. The citizens of Las Vegas started the push to separate from Lincoln County in 1908. A "Division Club" was created and E.W. was an active member. They worked on proposing the new boundaries for soon-to-be Clark County.

In 1909 Griffith attempted to establish a second local cemetery, about a mile and a half south of town. It proved to be too far out for the local residents and E.W. shut it down by the end of the year. Griffith then focused his full attention on the construction of his two-story cement building on Fremont, just west of 2nd Street (Golden Nugget Casino's location today). Excavation work began before Christmas. The lower floor would house stores with nice glass windows while upstairs would be used for meeting space, offices and apartments. His project had a hefty cost of $12,000. Planning, designing, and construction would take over one and a half years.

Griffith was hired in June of 1910 as an inspector for a new school building under construction. He also became president of the Vegas Gun Club which had frequent competitions down in Searchlight.

October 8, 1910, Las Vegas Age ad

Sometime in 1910, Clayson and Griffith split up their oil and fuel company. Clayson took over the coal business and E.W. got the oil division. E.W. would run ads in the local paper for his "Griffith Oil and Fuel Co.".

With the Griffith Building nearing completion in August of 1911 (with 75 feet of frontage on Fremont and 140 feet on 2nd Street), businesses were lining up to sign leases. Walter Bracken, postmaster, was searching for larger quarters than what his post office had in the First State Bank. He leased the prime downstairs corner rooms at Fremont and 2nd. Just to the west, Cheney Drugs leased space. Griffith got creative and built a large theater upstairs. It was leased by the Majestic Theater and

Photo circa 1913 of the Griffith Building. The post office moved in at the corner downstairs and the Majestic Theater was located upstairs on the west end of the building.
Courtesy of the Clark County Museum

A photo circa 1915 of the lower level of the Griffith Building. The wide central opening was for the ticket booth and staircase of the Majestic Theater. The Las Vegas Age newspaper occupied quarters in the building just to the west.
UNLV Libraries, Special Collections

opened on April 20, 1912. Residents were delighted to have a nice theater to see silent films, plays and vaudeville acts from Los Angeles. It had 500 seats and on opening night the packed crowd gave E.W. a standing ovation in appreciation. The county's district attorney opened offices upstairs in 1912 as did local dentist Dr. Newell.

When Las Vegas officially became a city in 1911, a Chamber of Commerce was formed and E.W. would play a major role in its activities. As a member and also as its first president, Griffith would work on many committees. In those days, the Chamber was in charge of roads, their maintenance and development. In early 1913 work was done on improving a mile-and-a-half road leaving Las Vegas heading south. Griffith won election to a seat on the Clark County Commission and was put in charge of streets and public properties. He ordered studies for a car route from Utah to Las Vegas, which would require some form of bridge over the Virgin River. In September of 1913 E.W. went to Reno to represent the county at the State Fair. In November, the county began studying a possible road from Goodsprings to Las Vegas. Griffith was faithfully dedicated to improving roads in the city and county. He was also elected to the local Board of Education.

Undated photo circa 1920 in which the porch addition to the second floor along 2nd Street can be seen

In January of 1914, Governor Oddie sent E.W. to Dallas to represent the state at the National Corn Exhibition. In March of 1914 the Griffith Building sported a new white cement porch along the second floor facing 2nd Street. That summer Griffith filed to run for the State Assembly. He also travelled up to Kyle Canyon to search for land for an accessible mountain resort. While campaigning for the Assembly, E.W. pointed out his accomplishments to voters -- developing artesian wells, helping establish Clark County, assisting with the incorporation of Las Vegas, donating 40 books to the first school library, being president of the Chamber of Commerce, developing roads, building structures, and being a local businessman. Surprisingly, he lost in the November election.

Like many of the early Las Vegas businessmen, E.W. had a fascination with automobiles. In January of 1915 he returned home from Los Angeles in a new "Kisselkar" in just two days. Griffith was now on the Las Vegas City Commission. In May of 1915 E.W. located about 80 acres up in Kyle Canyon, about 40 miles outside of Las Vegas, for development as a summer resort. The altitude of over 7000 feet would mean much cooler summer days than in the city. There was plenty of runoff water from Mt. Charleston which could also generate electricity. He designed plans to build cabins. A road was already in progress to Tule Springs. Car travel to his property from Las Vegas would take about two hours but the return trip downhill only about 90 minutes. In June he ordered supplies to begin construction right away. He was able to open by July 4th and many prominent Las Vegans were among his first guests. Many visitors on the way there reported they could still see signs of the old Kyle Sawmill believed to be from the 1870's.

With the resort only open for summer business, E.W. spent the off months working on completing a direct road to his camp to shave six miles off the distance folks had to travel. His Charleston Resort became very popular and one day in August of 1916 he boasted he had 65 lodgers. The following year he had 125 guests one day in August with some folks having to sleep on the dining room floor or on the ground under the stars.

Like other successful businessmen in those days, Griffith would look for mining opportunities to invest in. In the summer of 1917, he was able to sell his "Dolly" group of mining claims (which he had with a partner) near Charleston Peak to the Yellow Pining Mine Co. for $20,000. He then took a 25% stake (for $10,000) in the Charleston Mining Co. which produced zinc.

Having served his city and county for over a decade, E.W. would decide to make another run for the Nevada State Assembly. He had lost in 1914 but in 1916 he was victorious, running as a Republican. He served two years. Son Robert had enrolled in 1917 at the University of Nevada in Reno.

In October of 1917 the Governor appointed E.W. to the National Civic Committee which held a convention in St. Louis. In March of 1918 Griffith went to California to purchase numerous pheasants for his mountain resort. He also announced that he was building a sawmill up in Kyle Canyon to produce lumber for more cabins at his resort.

Undated photo of
E.W. Griffith circa 1910's

Las Vegas Age photo of
son Robert Griffith

E.W. took his interest in roads very seriously. Now in the State Legislature where he leveraged some influence, he began studying potential routes to connect Corn Creek, Alamo, Ely and Pioche. Assemblyman Griffith served as both the Federal Food Administrator in Nevada and the Fuel Administrator for Clark and Lincoln Counties during WWI. He was also the President of the Southern Nevada Agricultural Board.

In June of 1918 E.W. decided to run for the State Senate as a Republican but would soon switch parties to run as an Independent in favor of Prohibition. In November of 1918 he won his race and would serve a four-year term in the Senate. Now as a Senator, in 1919 he continued to show enthusiasm towards the improvement of the state's roads. The rough route from Los Angeles to Salt Lake City was called the Arrowhead Trail. It passed through Searchlight on its way to Las Vegas. He sought to find other alternatives and pushed for a bridge over the Virgin River. He also was in favor of creating a road from Goldfield to Beatty and then on to Las Vegas using the abandoned Las Vegas & Tonopah Railroad route. The road from Las Vegas to Searchlight and then to the California border was improved. Griffith also pushed for improving the road from Las Vegas to Jean, Nevada. In May of 1919, a study was begun on how to connect Las Vegas to the Tahoe area. In late 1919 he was appointed to the new State Cement Board which began discussing the creation of a cement plant along with a smelter.

Before E.W. reopened his Mount Charleston Resort for the summer months of 1919, he did multiple improvements. A stage line from downtown Las Vegas to the resort was established. A one-way ticket was $2. Once open, E.W. advertised a weekly room rate of $5 and for an additional $10 food would be included. His resort offered music, dancing, a pool table, swings, evening fires, hiking, a beautiful environment and free parking. The more affluent people of Las Vegas made annual summer trips up to the resort to escape the heat below.

July 5, 1919, Las Vegas Age ad

Undated photo of a typical cabin up in Mt. Charleston
UNLV Libraries, Special Collections

Photo circa early 1920's of a car on the road up to Griffith's Mt. Charleston Resort
UNLV Libraries, Special Collections

In late 1919 E.W. purchased four lots in town adjacent to the Union Hotel on Main Street to open a lumber yard by springtime to sell his Charleston Peak lumber locally. His mountain sawmill was very active and productive.

In March of 1920, Griffith's mother Jane of Pasadena turned 100 years old. She was born in 1820 in Quebec, Canada. She would pass about a year later, just shy of her 101st birthday. (His dad had died in 1901.)

In October of 1920 E.W. married for the second time. His bride was Fletcher Midgley, formerly of Gadsden, Alabama. They wed in Los Angeles and made plans to build a home in Las Vegas. In June of 1921 the couple headed to New York to catch a boat to England where they would vacation. Upon his return, he entered into a construction contract to build a two-story building near his Griffith Building. As a Senator, he realized that there was work to be done to connect Las Vegas to Reno. There was no direct route. Car travelers had to choose between a 1,000-mile trip through Los Angeles or an even longer one through Salt Lake City. In December of 1921 Griffith was selected by the Las Vegas Chamber of Commerce to represent the city at the League of the Southwest meeting in California to discuss water and power on the Colorado River. In June of 1922 he was appointed to the National Highway Association due to his intense interest in the development of roadways in the West. He would also propose that the "Valley of Fire" become a National Monument.

E.W. was elected to serve again on the local School Board in 1922; a position he would keep for the rest of his life. That summer he decided to run for Lt. Governor but lost the election in November. With his four-year term in the Senate ending, his service in the State Legislature came to a conclusion.

In the summer of 1922, Griffith was awarded a $37,380 contract to build two school buildings on the same block as the grammar school.

The year 1923 saw E.W. buy mining property near his resort which was prospering. Some 250 people reserved resort cabins for July 4th. In September, he signed leases on numerous apartments over the post office in his Griffith Building.

In January of 1924, E.W. was hired by Dr. Roy Martin and William Ferron to build them a structure on Fremont Street which would become the Oasis Confectionary. That summer a pool, tennis court, and additional cabins were added to his resort.

Undated postcard photo of the cabin used as the office for the Mt. Charleston Resort
UNLV Libraries, Special Collections;
William Wright Photo Collection (0094 0018)

In March of 1925 E. W. made a run for mayor of Las Vegas but came in last. In August his son Robert (who was now postmaster) and wife Ruth gave E.W. a grandchild, a girl named Mary Jane. The next month, E.W. and his wife headed to Long Beach, California to take a year off and relax. He made a trip down to Mexico to view tracts of land. They moved to Hollywood for a while and E.W. made occasional trips back to Vegas for business and family visits. In May of 1926 Griffith announced plans to repair his sawmill which was three miles below his resort. It was in a heavy timber area and had not been operational for about two years. He wanted to add a mill to produce better quality timber. The county also agreed to improve seven miles of road in the area. Griffith also gave thought to building a resort hotel up in the mountains with lighting and water systems.

In July of 1927 E.W. started construction on a resort home up in the mountains for his family. The following summer he fell ill and had to be hospitalized. The nature of his ailment is unknown, but he recovered. In February of 1930 E.W. and his wife visited her native Alabama. Griffith took a side trip to Havana, Cuba. The new family log cabin up near the resort was completed by the summer of 1931. Phone service was then added to the resort.

Rotary club photo circa 1930 of E.W. Griffith
UNLV Libraries, Special Collections;
Sherwin Scoop Garside Photo Collection (0067 0016)

Griffith began to slow down in 1931 and decided to retire. He signed over all his holdings and operations to his son Robert. Robert had already purchased the Griffith building from his dad for $100,000 in 1929.

Two June 1929 photos are pieced together to show a complete view of the long front of the Griffith Building along Fremont. When the post office vacated its space on the corner in 1929, Robert opened his own tobacco shop.
UNLV Libraries, Special Collections; R.B. Griffith Photo Collection (0106 0001)

As E.W.'s health declined in the early 1930's, son Robert saw to his care. Griffith turned 70 on September 9, 1932, and passed away at his home at 226 South 2nd Street on October 31, 1932. He was buried beside family members in Pasadena. He second wife passed away one year later at the age of 63.

Undated Las Vegas Review Journal photo of Robert Griffith

Edmond W. Griffith was honored in 1955 when the Griffith United Methodist Church on E. Oakey Blvd. was named after him. In 1962 the Griffith Elementary School opened with 415 students; son Robert was at the dedication ceremony. We also have Griffith Peak in the mountains outside of town and the Mary Jane Falls which were named after his granddaughter.

Son Robert had a very distinguished career himself with many major accomplishments. While serving as postmaster in the late 1920's, he oversaw the start of home and business mail delivery. He helped establish Nellis Air Force Base and McCarran Field. He also supported the start of airmail service to Las Vegas. Robert Griffith was influential in the creation of the Lake Mead to Las Vegas water pipeline. He passed away in March of 1978 at age 79.

Edmond and his son Robert should be remembered for their vast contributions to Las Vegas, Clark County and the State of Nevada. Generations benefited from their hard work and accomplishments.

Chapter 14
William E. Hawkins
Merchant, Mayor, Developer, Public Servant

Despite being the second mayor of Las Vegas and having served for six years, William Edward Hawkins does not have much written about him.

William's father Augustine (who went by "Austin") was born September 21, 1825, in Ohio. In his younger years he was a steamboat operator on the Mississippi River. He moved to Yreka, California to try his hand at mining in August of 1849. William's mother, Bridgett McDonnell, was born in 1835 in Ireland and came to the United States by boat, traveling around Cape Horn. They were married on February 2, 1852, in Yreka, California which is about 20 miles below the Oregon border. Austin was the county clerk and helped found Masonic Lodge #1 in Northern California. He also served as the postmaster of Yreka for four years in the late 1890's. William was his first born on April 2, 1863. He was followed by four more children, all born in Yreka -- Norton in 1865, Cornelia in 1866, Robert in 1869 and Nellie in 1872. William attended public schools in Yreka.

Photo circa 1925 of William Hawkins
*UNLV Libraries, Special Collections;
Elizabeth Harrington Photo Collection (0291 0039)*

After doing some farming, William would leave the family home and moved to a small town, called Ager, about 15 miles northeast of Yreka. Ager was just shy of the California-Oregon border and was a stage and freight stop. In the late 1880's the Central Pacific Railroad was being built which helped Ager grow. There was a need for stores and William is known to have started the first general store there. He dealt in general merchandise as well as livestock. In early 1904 William sold his business and began liquidating his land holdings in Ager.

July 8, 1905, Las Vegas Times ad for Hawkins' store on Clark Ave. in McWilliams' Original Townsite

Why William decided to up and leave for Las Vegas in 1905 is not known. Hawkins was a registered guest at Ladd's tent Hotel on April 1, 1905. He opened a general store on Clark Avenue in a tent in J.T. McWilliams' Original Townsite to the west of the new railroad tracks (now the Westside of Las Vegas) in early 1905. Hawkins store sold shoes, boots, and men's clothing.

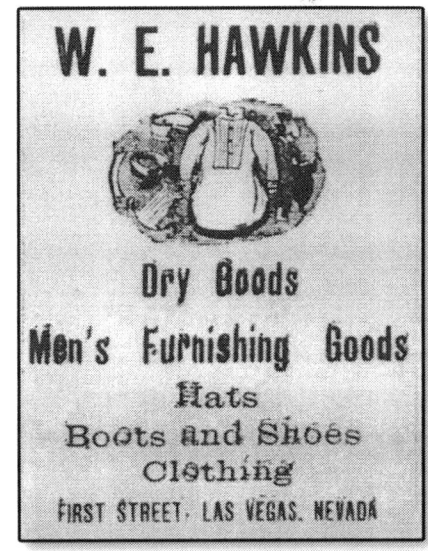
February 24, 1906, Las Vegas Age ad for Hawkins' store, now located on South First Street in the new railroad town

W.E. Hawkins participated in the May 1905 land auction conducted by a subsidiary of the railroad owned by wealthy Montana Senator William A. Clark. He purchased several lots and like numerous other merchants in McWilliams' town, William defected and relocated his store to the new railroad town of Las Vegas right after the auction. By the late summer of 1905 Hawkins was operating a store on 1st Street.

When residents recognized the need to explore sanitary conditions in the young town, William volunteered in June of 1905 to serve on a study committee. It would be his first step in a long career of public service.

Rare photo circa 1907 showing stores on the south side of Fremont Street. The Imperial Restaurant was on the southwest corner of 1st Street, followed by Shannon's Red Cross Drug Store, Fallas' General Merchandise Store and then Hawkins' store.
Courtesy of the Nevada State Museum, Las Vegas

In January of 1906 William moved his store off 1st Street to the south side of Fremont, just east of 1st Street. It was opposite the First State Bank that recently opened in a nice cement block building on the north side of Fremont. Hawkins' store sold general dry goods and furnishings. By March of 1906 Hawkins had purchased the inventory of two other businesses to consolidate with what he had. He became known as "The Merchant Prince of Southern Nevada".

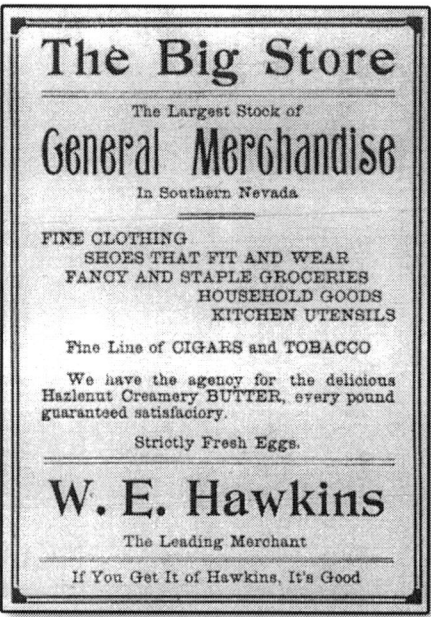

May 19, 1906, Las Vegas Times ad

July 28, 1906, Las Vegas Age ad

September 29, 1906, Las Vegas Age ad

August 31, 1907, Las Vegas Age ad

Las Vegas was part of Lincoln County and had representation on the county commission up in Pioche. In October of 1906 William ran to obtain that seat. In November he won by a vote of 145 to 17. He would make the long and tedious trip to Pioche whenever the commission scheduled a meeting.

In July of 1907 he improved ventilation in his Hawkins "Big Store" as it was known. Later that year, as a Lincoln County commissioner, he called for a larger proper town jail to be funded and built in Las Vegas.

Undated photo of the jail that was eventually constructed
after Clark County broke off from Lincoln County

October 8, 1910, Las Vegas Age ad

April 8, 1911, Las Vegas Age ad

June 17, 1911, Las Vegas Age ad

November 4, 1911, Las Vegas Age ad

In early 1908 William started another store on the north side of Fremont (two doors east of the bank), across the street from his current store on the south side. He divided his stock to fill both stores. The store on the north side concentrated on men's furnishing.

Sentiment was growing in 1908 to have Southern Nevada split from Lincoln County. The county seat at Pioche was just too far away and too difficult to get to when one needed to handle court, land or tax concerns. Locally, businessmen in Las Vegas formed the "Division Club" to commence studying the steps and logistics needed to form "Clark County". William joined the group. After the state of Nevada authorized the creation of the new county of Clark, William tendered his resignation from the Lincoln County Commission effective at the end of June 1909. The next day, on July 1 of 1909, the Governor appointed Hawkins as one of three brand new Clark County commissioners. He was chosen its chairman. William acquired stock in 1909 in the First State Bank and was appointed to its board of directors. In the election of 1910, he lost his county commissioner seat and directed his attention to his two stores.

In 1911, Judge William R. Thomas had completed a nice new cement structure named the Mesquite Building on the southeast corner of Fremont and 1st Street. William decided to lease space on the ground floor just to the east of Ralph Thomas' Mesquite Grocery store. He would consolidate the merchandise of his two locations into this one new store. Whatever grocery inventory he had, he sold to Ralph Thomas. His "New Store" would only sell dry goods, shoes, and clothes. The store had large plate glass windows and opened in May of 1911. His store near the bank was taken over by a meat market.

Las Vegas became a city in 1911 and folks wanted a mayor. Only two men stepped forward to run, William and Peter Buol. Buol won by 10 votes to become the first mayor of Las Vegas. William helped draft the city charter and when a Chamber of Commerce was formed, he became an active member. William initiated a contest to pick a city slogan and offered a $5 prize to the winner. The winning selection was "Las Vegas and its Valley -- An Empire in Itself".

Hawkins continued to run his store while serving as Mayor of Las Vegas. May 10, 1913, Las Vegas Age ad

In 1913 another election for mayor was conducted and this time Hawkins ran unopposed. With 329 votes, William was sworn in as the second mayor of Las Vegas on May 14. In 1914 he designated November 18 as "Clean-up Day". Schools were closed and many participated in cleaning alleys and backyards of trash and empty tin cans. Hawkins would be reelected twice and served as mayor for six consecutive years.

William would make frequent buying trips to Los Angeles to acquire summer and winter goods for his "New Store". William suffered from the Spanish Flu in 1918. He ended his three terms as mayor in June of 1919. His health would not be the best after he had the flu. In January of 1921, at the age of 57, he sold his business to Adcock & Ronnow. After almost 16 years of operating a store in Las Vegas, he retired and worked on getting back to health.

William never thought of marriage until he met Estella (Stella) Pauff who worked in his mercantile store. Stella was born in Ohio in 1876 and came with her parents and siblings to Las Vegas in 1906. Her brother Arthur arrived the year before and started a clothing store. Her father Peter was the Courthouse's janitor. William and Stella married on July 2, 1921, in Los Angeles and remained there to honeymoon. It was her second marriage. They would have no children.

W.E Hawkins was a very successful businessman who accumulated enough wealth to purchase a sizeable number of city lots (from the railroad) just south and east of town. After departing politics and retiring as a merchant, he turned to real estate and land development projects which were referred to as "Additions". Upon returning to Las Vegas after his honeymoon in 1921, he began his "Hawkins Addition" of some 200 lots located from Bridger to Stewart and from 5th (now Las Vegas Blvd.) to 7th Streets in a triangular-shaped parcel. William started the Hawkins Land and Water Company with Stella as its vice president. It was the first Las Vegas water company not owned by the railroad. Water would arrive to his lots in February of 1922. Sidewalks followed. William and Stella would build their own home at 5th and Ogden.

In late 1922 William accepted an appointment to the Las Vegas City Park Board to fill a vacancy. 1923 saw William become a member of the Nevada State Board of Equalization. From 1923 to 1925 he served as the Clark County Assessor.

In late 1924 Hawkins sold a 60-acre tract of unimproved land he held outside of town for $50 per acre. During the summer of 1926, Stella and William took a well-deserved one week vacation up to E.W. Griffith's Charleston Peak Resort up in Kyle Canyon. Soon thereafter, William began planning his next tract project, the "South Addition" of 240 lots which by 1929 was well underway. It stretched in an odd-shaped parcel from Garces to Charleston and from Main to 5th, plus a portion of land along 6th Street.

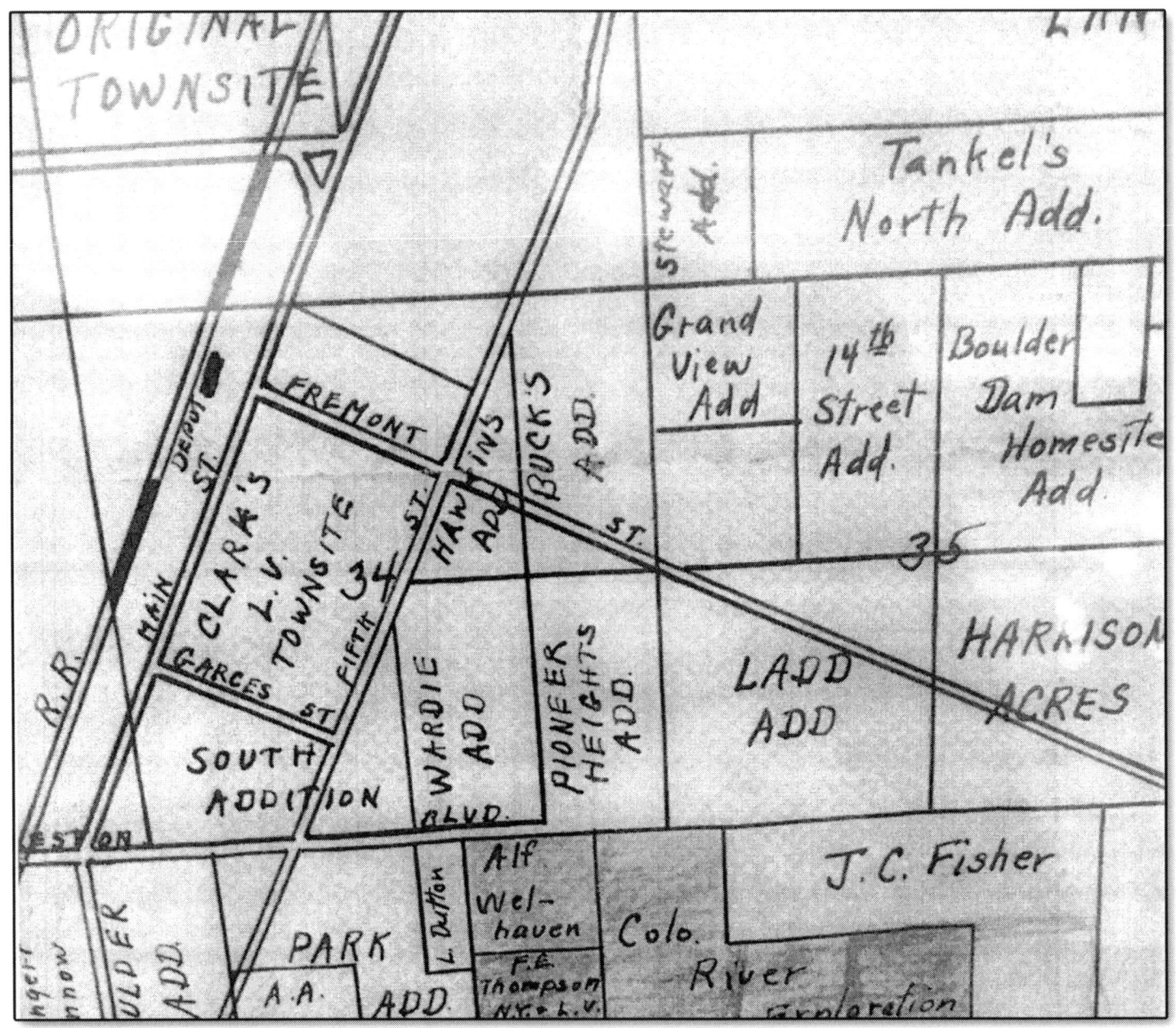

1936 land map of Las Vegas showing both of Hawkins' Additions. The first one, labeled "Hawkins Add", can be seen just left of center, just east of Fremont and Fifth Streets. The second one, labeled "South Addition" can be seen in the lower left corner of the map.
Clark County Museum map

In May of 1929 William accepted an appointment from Governor Balzar to the State Tax Commission which required him to make occasional 3 to 4 week trips to Carson City. Roads were notoriously poor in those days to the northern part of the state and travelers often had to travel through California. In September of 1930 on the way to a tax meeting, William fell very ill while visiting one of his sisters in Sacramento, California. Unable to carry out his duties on the State Tax Commission due to poor health, he resigned his seat. In October he had surgery in Sacramento and headed to Los Angeles in November to rest. He would return home to Las Vegas in December.

The 1930's were mostly quiet years for William as he oversaw his land and water projects while battling worsening arthritis. He and his wife resided at 131 No. 5th Street. Later in the decade his health would seriously decline. In August of 1939 William fell ill and had to be hospitalized. He was losing his long battle with arthritis. In June of 1940 his condition was critical. William Hawkins would pass away at age 77 on August 6, 1940, after being in the Las Vegas Hospital for almost a year. The cause of his death was attributed to a bad choking spell. William was buried in Woodlawn Cemetery. Pallbearers included prominent Las Vegas pioneers Walter Bracken, Ed Von Tobel Sr., and Charles "Pop" Squires. He was spoken highly of by his many fraternity brothers. William was just one of two active surviving 1905 founding Las Vegas Eagles members (he had membership card #2). He was also a Mason and an Elks lodge member.

Screenshot of W.E. Hawkins in a 1930 film done by William S. Park and Fred Wilson
UNLV Libraries, Special Collections;
"Views in and Around Las Vegas" (F849.L35 V54X)

Stella would take over management of William's land holdings after his death. In 1955 she leased the southeast corner of 5th and Ogden for $550 per month to the city to serve as a metered parking lot. In June of 1956 Stella celebrated her 50th anniversary of living in Las Vegas. In the summer of 1958 Stella would wed John Paul Jones in Northern Nevada. It was her third marriage. Her new husband had careers in the restaurant business and law enforcement. After their wedding they travelled to Lake Tahoe, San Francisco and San Diego before returning to live in Las Vegas. Stella would sell land on No. 5th Street to motel developers.

Las Vegas Review Journal photo of Stella Hawkins in the December 18, 1976, edition

In December of 1976 the city honored Stella on her 100th birthday. She was still mentally alert, with some decline in hearing and eyesight. Stella still lived at home with some daily assistance. She would pass at the Charleston Convalescent Center on December 11, 1978, just days shy of her 102nd birthday. Having outlived her siblings and having no children, a large portion of her estate was donated to UNLV. She was buried in Woodlawn Cemetery next to William.

William Edward Hawkins achieved many goals during his lifetime. He was a successful merchant, a commissioner of both Lincoln and Clark Counties, a bank director, a mayor of Las Vegas for six years, a major land developer, a County Assessor, a member of the State Board of Equalization and the Tax Commission, a member of the Las Vegas Chamber of Commerce and a dedicated member of numerous local fraternities. He loved and served faithfully his city, his county, and his state.

Chapter 15
Dr. Roy Martin
Physician, Businessman, Investor and Public Servant

When a new town is created in quick fashion there is an almost immediate need for basic services such as banking, utilities, lawyers and judges, lodging, law enforcement, barbers and general stores. Another prime necessity is medical services. As Las Vegas sprung out of heat, dust and wind in May of 1905, people looked to the railroad to meet many of those needs. The San Pedro - Los Angeles - Salt Lake Railroad had numerous workers in the Las Vegas valley in late 1904 and early 1905 that needed medical attention, so it was only natural that the first doctors and hospitals in the area had direct ties to the railroad. Dr. Roy Wood Martin did not arrive until August of 1905, about three months after the railroad's land auction. Who was Dr. Martin and how did he come to be a principal player in the field of medicine in early Las Vegas?

Undated photo of Dr. Roy Martin

Dr. Martin had his roots in Nebraska and was born on November 11, 1874. His parents were Gabriel Royse Martin (1846 - 1907) and Phila Amelia Martin (1844 - 1914). They married in Table Rock, Nebraska in 1872 and that is where they raised their family of six children. Even though his given name was Royce (note his father's middle name was Royse and in some writings Dr. Martin is actually referred to as Royse as opposed to Royce), he preferred to go by Roy.

Photo circa 1906 of Roy's parents
Ancestry.org photo

Roy's father was a Nebraska farmer and later a general merchant dealing in dry goods and grains. He also was a livestock broker and operated a meat market. As a youngster, Roy worked for his dad.

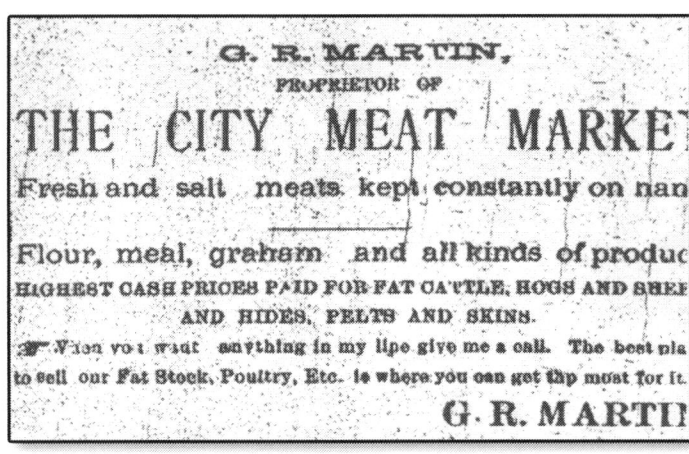

Undated Nebraska newspaper ad for
Roy's father's store in Table Rock, Nebraska

Undated photo of the Martin house in Nebraska
Ancestry.org photo

After completing high school in Table Rock, Roy attended Wesleyan University for one year. In 1898 he obtained a degree from the Omaha College of Business. He then attended University Medical College in Kansas City, Missouri where he obtained his medical degree in 1903. While in medical school he would frequent Beaver County (in the panhandle of the Oklahoma Territory) to check out real estate opportunities. One summer he made a trip to explore the west coast.

Upon graduating medical school, Roy went to Monterey, Mexico where he served as a yellow fever quarantine officer. He contracted the disease himself which forced his return to Oklahoma in 1904 where he practiced medicine for about a year. Hearing about successful ore strikes in Goldfield, Nevada he had the itch to head west. His journey to Goldfield had him stop in the new town of Las Vegas in August of 1905. While there he learned that the rush in Goldfield was subsiding and thus decided to remain in Las Vegas.

There is a popular tale that there was a doctor already in town who was anxious to leave. He was ready to sell his practice and supplies for just $10. Roy was interested but didn't have the funds. So according to the tale, he put out the word that he was willing to have a foot race with anyone, with the loser paying the winner $10. Roy was a good runner and naturally won, allowing him to begin his long medical career in Las Vegas.

A 1904 photo of the tent used by the railroad as a temporary hospital
UNLV libraries, Special Collections

Photo circa mid-1880's of a young Halle Lincoln Hewetson who would become one of the earliest doctors in Las Vegas
Find A Grave photo

Upon nearing completion of the tracks in Las Vegas the railroad opened a tent hospital near the area where a depot would be built. It was staffed by Dr. Halle Hewetson who came to the region in late 1904 to seek relief from a lung affliction. He would move the hospital into quarters of the new Las Vegas Land and Water Co. building located nearby on Main Street. He would remain the railroad's principal doctor in Las Vegas for many years.

It is believed Dr. Martin's first practice was in an 8 by 10 foot tent located at Stewart and 3rd Streets. His second location was a temporary one in October of 1905 in part of a two-story wooden structure that had been used by the First State Bank for a short period on Fremont Street, between 1st and 2nd Streets. Some four months after arriving, Dr. Martin was appointed chief surgeon of the newly forming Las Vegas - Tonopah Railway (a position he would keep for about 12 years).

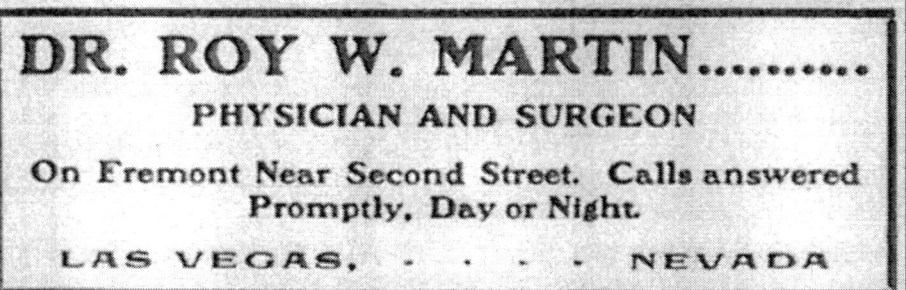

A March 31, 1906, Las Vegas Times ad run by Dr. Martin

In early 1906 the SP - LA - SL Railroad hired Dr. Martin as a doctor and surgeon. He started with one patient in March and was asked to oversee with Dr. Hewetson the medical concerns of some 300 railroad employees in the area. He was also responsible for caring for workers in Tonopah. Serious cases that they couldn't address had to be transported to Los Angeles by train.

In June of 1906 Judge William Thomas was nearing completion of his beautiful cement two-story structure on the northwest corner of Fremont and 1st Street. Roy along with two partners, Dan Noland and William Wilson, leased most of the first floor to open a pharmacy. Wilson was president and operating manager while Nolan became secretary/treasurer. The men bought out the Shannon Red Cross and Hawkins Drug Stores to stock their new venture which they called "Wilson Drugs". They ordered counters, fixtures, supplies and equipment. The store had nice plate glass windows. Partner Roy opened a medical practice on the second floor to serve railroad employees, day and night.

The Thomas Block building at Fremont and 1st Streets. Undated photo.
UNLV Libraries, Special Collections

In January of 1907 Dr. Martin took a leap and leased most of the still vacant second floor of the Thomas Building to start his "Las Vegas Hospital". He organized it to have an operating room, a drug room and private patient rooms. He installed 12 beds and hired a nurse. He would not treat infectious diseases. Folks residing outside of town were welcome to come and seek medical attention at his facility. Roy quickly became known as a doctor willing to travel afar to treat people in need, making occasional trips to mining camps. He rode a buckboard to distant areas such as Death Valley and Goldfield. He also treated local Indians and looked after the ladies of the night in the brothels of Block 16.

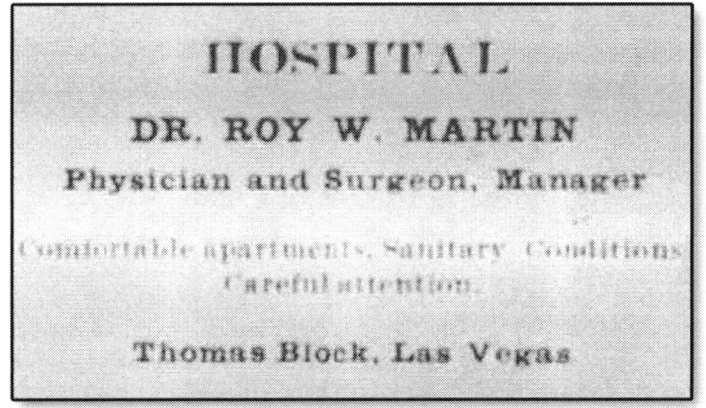

February 2, 1907, Las Vegas Age ad

In May of 1907 Dr. Martin accepted an appointment as the Lincoln County doctor which paid one dollar per year. It was a position of esteem.

When telephone service arrived in Las Vegas by early 1908, Roy's hospital received telephone number 6. In April of the next year Roy purchased three lots along Main Street with the intention of tearing down the simple buildings on them to build a hospital. That hospital was never built. In 1909 Dr. Martin struck a deal with the county to see to the medical needs of local prisoners.

An undated photo of the northeast corner of Fremont and 2nd Streets where cement bricks were produced for use in local building construction
UNLV Libraries, Special Collections

With a steady income coming in from his medical and hospital businesses, Roy was flush with cash and began investing in more real estate. In March of 1910 he partnered with William Wilson to go on a buying spree. They first purchased a lot on Fremont Street between 1st and 2nd Streets for $1350. Then they bought four prime lots on the northeast corner of Fremont and 2nd Streets for $6000 from Chris Brown. That was the biggest purchase of land in town since the 1905 auction. The corner was being used as a cement block production yard. Finally, they went after a section of land about four miles east of town.

In September of 1909 Roy married 34-year-old Nelle ("Nellie") Charlotte Cotton in Seward, Nebraska. Upon returning to Las Vegas, the newlyweds were honored with a gala affair at the Opera House. Nellie had attended two music colleges and was a talented pianist and organist. She would often show off her talents in local musical performances. That summer Roy purchased two lots from the Las Vegas Improvement Co. on the southwest corner of Fremont and 5th Streets for $700 to build a home for Nellie. Their house had six rooms and was composed of cement blocks. It had an eight-foot porch supported by heavy columns. Roy and Nellie moved into their new home in February of 1911. (It was razed in 1932 for a Standard Oil service station.) In March of 1911 a Dr. H.H. Clark joined Roy as a partner at the hospital above the pharmacy at Fremont and 1st. They began doing some remodeling which included installation of a heating system, electrical fans and appliances, and a kitchen so patients could be served proper meals. Roy started his long association with the Chamber of Commerce (which he had helped organize in 1910) where he began his push for road construction. He also became very active with the small Republican Party in Las Vegas. In May he partnered with Mr. and Mrs. E.S. Wharton to buy out the Wilson Pharmacy below his hospital. It became the Wharton Drug Company.

A 1918 photo of Roy's wife Nellie
UNLV Libraries, Special Collections

A 1930 photo of Frances Martin when she was about 19 years old
Ancestry.org photo

In July of 1911, Nellie and Roy had their first child, a girl named Frances. A year later Roy became the vice-president of the newly formed Las Vegas Homebuilders.

Mazie Martin in 1930 at about age 17
Ancestry.org photo

They ordered a concrete mixer and made plans to build four and five room cottages in town. In December of 1912 Roy was elected vice-president of the Chamber of Commerce. A month later in January of 1913, Roy and partner C.C. Ronnow sold their "Bishop Gypsum" property about six miles northeast of Las Vegas. In September, the Martin's had their second and final child, a daughter named Phila "Mazie".

In April of 1914 the Wharton's sold out their share of the pharmacy to Dr. Martin due to poor health and moved to Louisiana. In October Roy partnered with Judge Thomas to buy the Herman Sund Section west of town for $10,000. It already had an operating artesian well. In December Roy was elected president of the Chamber of Commerce, a title which he would keep for years.

Dr. Martin's hospital partner, Dr. H.H. Clark, sold back his interest in the hospital to Roy in January of 1915 and moved to Gallup, New Mexico. Roy's brother Dr. Charles Martin then arrived in town to work with Roy. In August they were joined by a Dr. Gill from Kansas. In October Roy added a second story to his home. It contained two bedrooms, closets and a storeroom.

In March of 1916 Dr. Martin built the first hospital in Goodsprings, Nevada. He placed a Dr. Thomas in charge. In June of 1916 Roy and partner Judge William R. Thomas sold their Sund Section of land to L. Lindsey of Los Angeles for a nice profit.

In January of 1917 a Dr. Weise from North Dakota joined the hospital's staff. Roy continued to be under contract with Clark County to care for the indigent population of the area. In the

Undated photo of the Martin's two-story home at Fremont and Fifth Streets
UNLV Libraries, Special Collections

spring of 1917 Roy purchased lots for $10,000 at one of the corners of 2nd and Ogden for a proposed "Las Vegas General Hospital". He made plans for a Spanish-style two story structure measuring 45 by 85 feet. It would have a kitchen, laundry, steam plant, patient wards, offices, operating room, x-ray room, and a sterilizing room. It would have the capacity to house 30 patients. For some unknown reason it never came to be.

In May of 1918 a Dr. Lewis from New York joined the hospital's staff. That July Roy went on a road trip with his wife, one of his young daughters along with one of her friends to Caliente. After departing Hiko they ran out of gas. Roy left the group to go by foot to find food, water and gas. The road in the area was not well defined and at one point Roy mistakenly began to backtrack during his journey. He fell asleep and had hallucinations in the desert heat. Luckily, he found a source of water which cleared his head. He was gone 28 hours before returning with food, water and gas. The ladies were unable to locate water on their own and his daughter recalled later in life licking moisture drops off the hood of their car waiting for her dad to return. They were hungry, hot and dehydrated. They were thrilled to see Roy again and the party safely made their way on to Caliente.

When the Spanish Influenza was wreaking havoc in the world in 1918, Dr. Martin was the Chief Health Officer of Clark County. He had twelve beds to treat the ill. He advised residents to avoid crowds, keep apart from others, wear masks, isolate at home, when possible, bathe often, brush their teeth frequently and gargle with antiseptic.

In late 1917 Dr. Martin purchased the wooden Palace Hotel on No. 2nd Street for $10,000 to reconfigure as a hospital. The sale included two adjacent cottages, shade trees and a nice rear yard. The Palace Hotel was the first two story wooden structure built in Las Vegas. Roy began redoing the interior, changing wooden walls to ones of plaster. He installed equipment and 12 beds for patients. He built an operating room, a maternity ward, an x-ray room, and a nursery. A steam plant and an elevator were installed. An exterior veranda was added on. Roy brought in Dr. Forrest Mildren and Dr. F. M. Ferguson to assist. The doctors were seeing about five influenza patients arrive every day at the hospital above the pharmacy at 1st and Fremont while the new one was being fitted. As deaths increased into the fall, Roy advised the county to keep the schools closed. He also called for all chairs be removed from lobbies, pool halls, churches and theaters. Bans were lifted by early December.

Undated photo of the previous Palace Hotel that Dr. Martin purchased and converted into a hospital
UNLV Libraries, Special Collections

Undated photo of Dr. Forrest Mildren (right) alongside Las Vegas Age editor and publisher Charles "Pop" Squires
UNLV Libraries, Special Collections

LAS VEGAS HOSPITAL
Trained Nurses in constant attendance. Laboratory. X-Ray. Fully equipped to handle both Medical and Surgical cases.
ROY W. MARTIN, M. D.
Physician & Surgeon
New Hospital Bldg.   Second St.

June 28, 1919, Las Vegas Age ad

In January of 1919 Roy's hospital was ready to open. It contained eight private patient rooms upstairs. He created a separate structure to handle county mental health patients, with a "Nut Box" designed to serve as a "Psychopathic Observation Ward". In January of 1919 the hospital's operation moved from above the pharmacy on Fremont and 1st Streets to its new location (the old upstairs space then became the Oak Hotel). Dr. Martin was able to treat cases of poisoning, pneumonia, and influenza.

The year 1919 saw Roy expand his mining interests. He became the president of the Waterville Mining and Milling Co. in Nelson. He also became the principal stockholder in the Divide Mining Co. which was about two miles outside of the Klondike area. Roy also invested in the Lincoln County Silver Mine.

In October of 1919 the Martin's along with Las Vegas Age newspaper owner "Pop" Squires went on a 1650-mile auto trip throughout Nevada and California in Roy's new Hudson Six Speedster sedan.

Roy had taken on Bill Ferron, a druggist, as a partner in the pharmacy at Fremont and 1st Streets. Later on they also owned the White Cross Drug Store at 2nd and Fremont.

In December of 1921 Dr. Martin went to a "League of the Southwest" meeting in Los Angeles to represent the Las Vegas Chamber of Commerce. Water and power concerns related to the Colorado River were discussed.

In early 1923 Roy decided to give politics a try. He entered the race for a seat in the State Assembly as a Republican and was successful. He moved the family to Carson City to be close to him while he served a few months in the State Legislature. He was on the Roads and Highway Committee where he proposed a more direct road between Los Angeles and Las Vegas. (Decades later it was more or less the route chosen for the I-15 Freeway). He did not seek reelection for a second term but did run for mayor of Las Vegas in May of 1923. He lost, coming in second out of five candidates.

In 1924, more rooms were added to his hospital and the interior was redecorated. In early 1925 Roy became chairman of the Las Vegas Businessmen's Association.

Roy purchased many new cars during his adult lifetime. He loved taking long road trips to see how well the cars performed, often timing his trips. In December of 1926 he had purchased a new Cadillac in Reno and was driving to Los Angeles with the Governor, a State Senator and an architect when his car began to skid just outside of Los Angeles on a wet road and flipped. The Governor was hospitalized for a few days with a sprained back. Roy fortunately was unhurt.

Rotary Club photo of Dr. Martin in the early 1920's
UNLV Libraries, Special Collections

In January of 1927 Dr. Martin served on a Nevada Commission to discuss a proposed dam project on the Colorado River. In April he began drawing up plans to build a three or four story building at a cost of $100,000 on his lots on the northeast corner of 2nd and Fremont. His plans changed and he sold the corner for $30,000 to wealthy Nevada banker George Wingfield for a hotel he wanted to build (but never did).

In early 1928 Dr. Martin was a member of the Colorado River Commission and flew by plane (he was seen off by many at the airfield in Las Vegas) to Chicago and Pittsburgh and then on to a Washington, D.C. meeting by train. In December of that year Roy ended his long run as president of the Las Vegas Chamber of Commerce.

In January of 1929 Roy became the president of a new group that was forming -- the Security Building & Loan Association. In February Roy and partners sold 80 acres near Fremont and 14th Street for $75,000. By this time Roy was also serving as President of the Boulder Realty Corporation (which was formed in 1926). In March Roy had the honor of listening in on the first long distance phone call made from Las Vegas. In April the Las Vegas Stock Exchange was forming and Roy was selected to lead its ten-member board of governors. With a partner he formed the Pursel-Martin Brokerage Company. Roy also became president of Associated Metals, Inc. which would restart mining of zinc and silver at Mt. Potosi. In May the company took over the old Diamond Queen Mining Company.

January 22, 1929, Las Vegas Age initial architect's drawing of Dr. Martin's proposed hospital

In July of 1929 Dr. Martin began plans for a new two-story hospital using stone from Death Valley. He wanted it to be north of Fremont and somewhere east of 5th Street. Earlier he was thinking of constructing it on his lots on the corner of Fremont and 2nd Streets. He would soon change the location again.

Dr. Martin was elected President of the Las Vegas Real Estate Board in February of 1930. In July he was chosen president of a new civic group called the "Greater Las Vegas Club". Its purpose was to spread the word about Las Vegas and the coming Boulder Dam.

In March of 1931 Dr. Martin sold his half interest in multiple drug stores to partner Bill Ferron to raise funds for his new hospital project which would help care for Boulder Dam project workers. He bought 16 lots on No. 8th Street between Ogden and Stewart as the site so his hospital would also be close to the center of town. Construction on a $100,000 building began in September. Roy partnered with Dr. Ferguson and Dr. Balcom to form the Las Vegas Hospital Association which would oversee the new hospital. They flipped coins to see who would be which officer. Roy became president and took on the cost of construction. His partners had the responsibility of purchasing fittings, equipment and supplies.

Undated photo of Dr. Martin, circa early 1930's
Courtesy of the Nevada State Museum, Las Vegas

A 1930 photo of Nellie Martin
Ancestry.org photo

In May of 1931, Roy sold his lots on the northwest corner of 2nd and Fremont to P.O. Silvagni of Utah for $30,000 for his 100 room Apache Hotel project.

Roy's new hospital made of stucco covered blocks with a red tiled roof opened on December 29, 1931. Over 1600 guests toured the facilities. Patients of Drs. Ferguson and Balcom transferred over. The hospital was the most modern one in the state and had a lab, a maternity ward, exam rooms, an operating room, an emergency room, and a medical library. It was built in the Mission Revival style and could handle between 40 and 60 patients. (The hospital closed in 1976 and the structure burned down in 1988.)

Undated newspaper photo of the hospital just after completion

Another photo of the hospital taken some time after it had opened
UNLV Libraries, Special Collections; Glenn Davis Photo Collection (0020 0006)

LAS VEGAS HOSPITAL ASSOCIATION
F. M. FERGUSON, M.D.   R. D. BALCOM, M.D.
J. R. McDANIEL, Jr., M.D.   ROY W. MARTIN, M.D.
New Las Vegas Hospital
EIGHTH AND OGDEN STREETS

February 17, 1932 Las Vegas Age ad

In 1937 Dr. Martin sold out his interest in the hospital. He was having financial troubles as he was unable to collect on some $80,000 in debt owed him. He still owned the old hospital on North 2nd Street which he then rejoined to generate some income. Due to a housing shortage in Las Vegas at the time, he turned the side yard, patio and cottages on the grounds of the hospital into the El Patio Hotel. (The hospital and hotel were eventually torn down to make room for a parking garage for the Fremont Hotel.)

In 1938 Roy was elected chairman of the Clark County Republican Central Committee. Also in 1938 Roy, with partners, took over the large Tintic Mine in Chloride, Arizona.

Dr. Martin owned 640 acres of land north of town with partners that they sold in 1941 to the U.S. Government for $25 per acre for a military training base (later to be become part of Nellis AFB). In 1941 Roy retired from running the El Patio Hotel. In a 1978 oral interview at UNLV, daughter Mazie recalled the family then moving to live on Roy's Harris Springs Ranch up on Mt. Charleston. Roy had homesteaded the property back in 1927 with James Cashman. It took some 10 years to get proper ownership documents completed. There were a few structures, but none had running water or electricity. Mazie remembered her sister Frances joining them after her husband entered the Army. They lived there about a year before leaving.

Undated photo of Dr. Martin with Alta Ham
UNLV Libraries, Special Collections;
Dokter Photo Collection (0012 0041)

With WWII still raging in Europe and the Pacific, there was a doctor shortage in the United States. Roy came out of retirement in late April of 1943 to work at the Basic Hospital in Henderson. He treated patients and also handled exams for incoming employees of the Basic Magnesium plant. The family lived in a house on Victory Drive in the young Basic townsite.

On November 27, 1943, Dr. Martin suffered a major heart attack. He spent three weeks in the Basic Hospital and was able to return home to continue his recovery. Unfortunately, he experienced two more debilitating heart attacks and died on December 22 at age 69. Roy was buried in Woodlawn Cemetery. He left numerous pieces of property to wife Nellie and his two daughters.

In late August of 1955 Nellie Martin suffered a serious stroke and was hospitalized for some two weeks. She had not been in the best of health for a couple of years. She would fall into a coma and die on November 2, 1955, at age 76. Nellie was also buried in Woodlawn.

A Las Vegas middle school was named in Dr. Roy Martin's honor in 1959.

Younger daughter Mazie had married James Jones in 1936. He became a WWII pilot. Mazie was a caseworker for many years for the Nevada State Welfare Department and passed away in Las Vegas in May of 1984 at age 70.

Woodlawn Cemetery grave marker for Dr. Martin
Find A Grave

Older daughter Frances married Richard Donnelly in 1935. He was a professor of criminal law and was a U.S. Army officer in WWII. They resided in Louisville, Kentucky and had five children. Frances passed away in May of 2009 at age 98 in North Madison, Connecticut where she was buried.

Dr. Roy Martin was a most prominent and respected Las Vegas citizen. He was a pioneer doctor and surgeon who went on to invest in pharmacies and hospitals. He dabbled in mining interests, real estate and politics. He served in the State Legislature and with the local Chamber of Commerce. He was president of many organizations and companies. Over his lifetime he invested in many businesses. Roy traveled far and wide to treat patients, never hesitating to visit mines and outlying ranches. He was a charter member of the Elks, the Rotary Club, the Masons and the Eagles. He was also a Shriner and was very actively involved with the local Republican party. He considered himself a great cheerleader for Las Vegas; one of its main "goodwill ambassadors". His daughter Mazie recalled he had but one vice -- his love of Lucky Strike cigarettes. Given his vast array of accomplishments and vital services to the Las Vegas community, Dr. Roy Martin shall be remembered as one of its most significant and distinguished citizens.

Chapter 16
William Ewart Ferron
Pharmacist, Businessman, Mayor

William Ferron did not arrive in Las Vegas until over a decade after the land auction was conducted.

William Ewart Ferron (named after William Ewart Gladstone, a Prime Minister of England) was born on February 23, 1887, in Salt Lake City, Utah. His father, Augustus Daniel Ferron, was born in Germany in 1847. His mother, Helene Salomon Ferron, was born in 1859 and was twelve years younger than Augustus. William's grandfather served with General Grant in the Civil War and afterwards Grant appointed him as Surveyor-General of Utah. Augustus Ferron, a civil engineer, did mineral surveys in Utah for the federal government and in the late 1860's to the early 1870's did land surveying in the Castle Valley area of Utah under the Homestead Act.

Undated photo (circa 1920's) of Augustus Ferron
Ancestry.org

An 1885 photo of William's mother Helene when she was 26 years old
Ancestry.org

Helene and Augustus had five children. Their first child, Henrietta, was born in 1881. She was followed by Frederick (1883), Edward (1885), William (1887), and Robert (1892). After graduating high school in 1904 in Salt Lake City, William headed to the Philadelphia College of Pharmacy where he obtained a degree in 1909. He then returned to Salt Lake City and with a friend opened a small pharmacy in the summer of 1910 that failed a year later. He then worked for a few years for a wholesale pharmaceutical company. Showing his desire to seek adventure, in 1913 William followed his brother Robert to Columbia, South America where he was involved in merchandising mining supplies. A bout of malaria forced him to return to the United States in 1916.

William Ferron first arrived in Las Vegas in July of 1916 and found lodging in the Charleston Hotel on 1st Street. It was a time when the population of Las Vegas was about 2,500 and most streets were still unpaved. Telephone service was available only during the day and electricity was shut off during the night. On a return trip to Salt Lake City that year he met Ruth Mary Cooper. Ruth was born July 20, 1893, in Minneapolis, Minnesota but grew

Undated photo (circa 1905) of William Ferron as a young man
Ancestry.org

up in Salt Lake City. After graduating the University of Utah, she taught elementary school in various Utah towns. Her father was co-owner of the Polk Publishing Co. which was the largest publisher of town directories in the United States. William and Ruth wed on February 7, 1917, and then travelled to California to honeymoon. Afterwards they headed to dusty Las Vegas to live in a small four-room rented home on 3rd Street.

Since its start in 1905, Las Vegas had numerous drug stores. The largest and most prominent pharmacy in town was inside the permanent solid block building on the northwest corner of Fremont and First Streets (the new Circa resort property today) which was constructed by Judge W.R. Thomas in 1906. The lower floor was initially leased to serve as a pharmacy by Dan Noland, W.B. Wilson and Dr. Roy Martin in November of 1906. Ownership of the pharmacy would change hands numerous times in the years ahead. In early 1910 Wilson sold his interest in the pharmacy to a Dr. Hanson of Los Angeles. Dr. Martin would buy out Hanson and Noland later that year and in May of 1911 would take on new partners, Mr. And Mrs. E.S. Wharton. Three years later in April of

A December, 1916 Salt Lake Tribune newspaper photo of Ruth Mary Cooper

1914, Dr. Martin would buy out the Wharton's and called his business the Las Vegas Pharmacy. He had been operating a small hospital on the second floor. Wanting to focus more on the hospital, Dr. Martin would sell his half-interest in the pharmacy to W.K. Kinnear, a druggist from San Diego who was already managing the business. Dr. Martin would then buy back Kinnear's interest and advertise for a new partner. William Ferron responded to the ad and Dr. Martin travelled to Salt Lake City to meet him. They got along and became equal partners in the pharmacy in 1916. In those days, drugs were prepared by hand by Ferron; few ready-to-sell drugs were available. The Las Vegas Pharmacy would become a regular advertiser in the Las Vegas Age newspaper.

An undated photo of the Thomas Building at the northwest corner of Fremont and 1st Streets. The pharmacy occupied the portion of the first floor on the left that faced Fremont Street.
UNLV Libraries, Special Collections

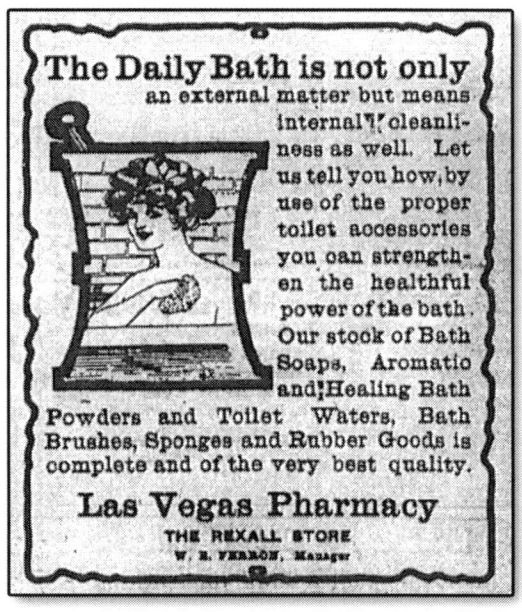

June 9, 1917 Las Vegas Age ad

October 13, 1917, Las Vegas Age ad

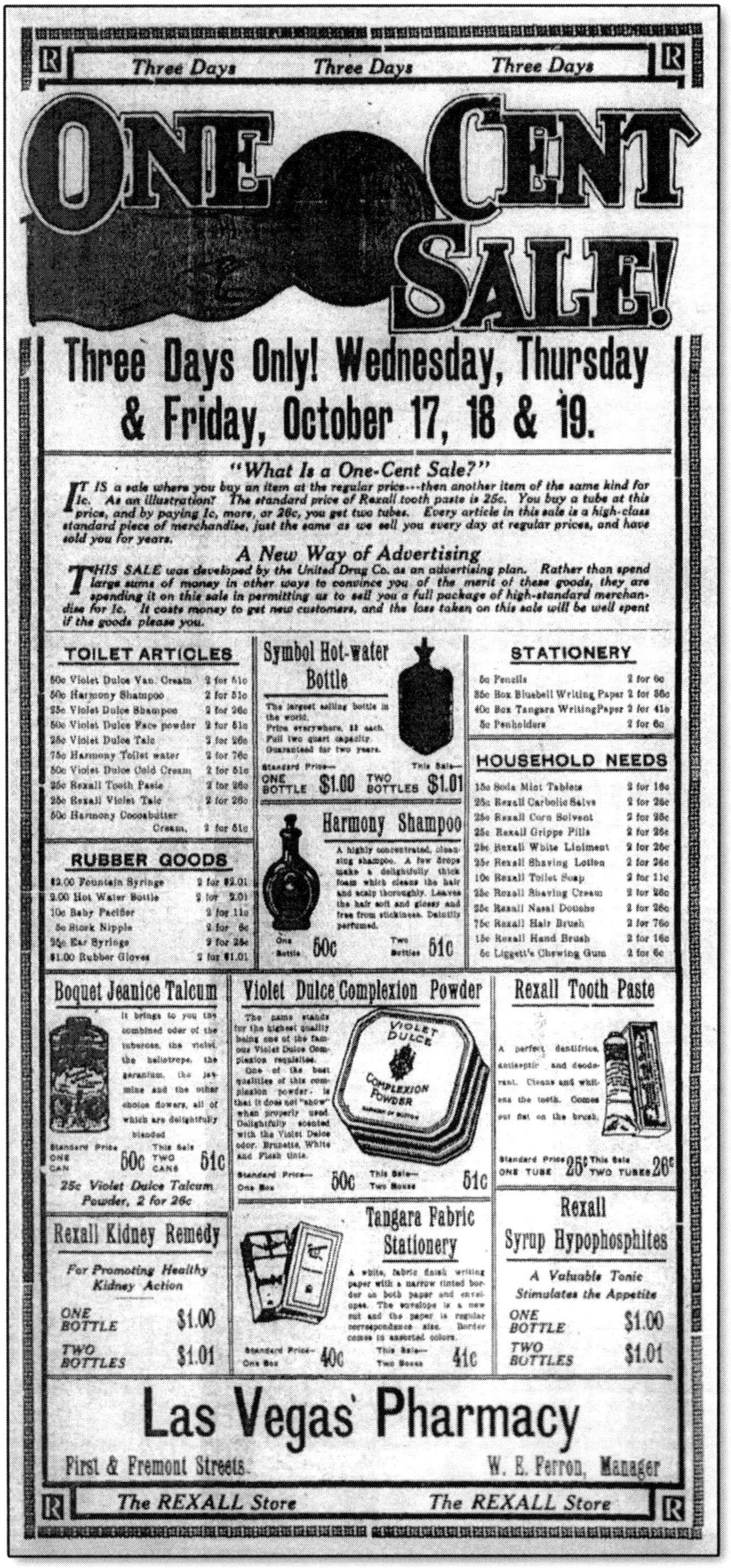

Ferron and Dr. Roy Martin purchased the manganese "Three Kids Mine" that was located in what is now present-day Henderson. They sold it for a profit a few years later.

In March of 1918, William and Ruth had their first child, Barbara, while in Los Angeles. The Ferron's lived in a small,

An undated photo circa 1920 of William's first born
Photo courtesy of the Clark County Museum

October 1919, Las Vegas Age ad

Undated photo of banker John S. Park's home on Fremont St. that was purchased by the Ferron family
UNLV Libraries, Special Collections

leased home near Fremont and 5th Streets until May of 1918 when they purchased (at the northeast corner of Fremont and 4th Streets) the larger and nicer home of John S. Park, the prominent town banker. Park had purchased the nearby old Kiel Ranch in 1911 where he built a beautiful summer home called the White House. When he finally decided to give up his home in town, the Ferron's were eager buyers paying a hefty $5,500.

In June of 1918 William was appointed the enrolling agent in Las Vegas for the U.S. Shipping Board. Young men from 21 to 30 years of age could come to William at the pharmacy to enroll in the Merchant Marines, which would exempt them from the WWI military draft.

Undated photo (circa 1921) of baby Shirley Ferron
Courtesy of Clark County Museum

Rotary Club photo circa early 1920's of William Ferron
UNLV Libraries, Special Collections

Undated photo circa 1920's of Ruth and William Ferron
UNLV Libraries, Special Collections

Las Vegas became a city in 1911. Its first mayor was Peter Buol (1911-1913) and the second mayor was W.E. Hawkins (1913-1919). In April of 1919 William Ferron entered the race to become the next mayor. When nobody filed to run against him, he automatically became the third mayor. On December 15, 1919, his second daughter, Shirley, was born. In 1920 he helped create the city's health board which would be in charge of enforcing any quarantines as well as combating the spread of contagious and infectious diseases (the deadly influenza pandemic had recently subsided). During his time in office William worked to pave more streets, place lighting in the McWilliams townsite on the west side of the railroad tracks, purchase better firefighting equipment and improve garbage removal. He also arranged for the city to have a night marshal on duty and a sheriff patrolling during the day. His term in office overlapped with the ugly Union Pacific Railroad strike. William ran for a second two-year term in May of 1921. He ran on a ticket with other local businessmen. They were up against the Shopmen's Ticket which was comprised of railroad employees. On May 3, 1921, H.T. Jones (a blacksmith foreman for the railroad) beat Ferron by a large margin (382 to 220) to become the city's fourth mayor. Ferron's last day in office was June 1, 1921. His brief venture into politics came to an end.

Like many other well-off early businessmen in Las Vegas, William had a fascination with automobiles and loved testing them on the primitive roads in those early days. In 1918 he purchased a Hupmobile, a car manufactured in Detroit. In 1920 he bragged of being able to drive from Caliente to Las Vegas in a record eight hours and thirty minutes. The family would often escape the hot Las Vegas summers by spending time in the cooler California locales of Long Beach, Santa Monica, and Laguna.

William also owned pharmacies out of town. He was a partner with Dr. Martin in the Pioche Pharmacy which they sold in 1920. He also owned the Caliente Drug Store which he sold in 1921. Both pharmacies were sold as they proved to be just too far away to properly oversee. William also owned stock in Lincoln County mining operations as well as undeveloped acreage about six miles outside of Las Vegas.

In 1920 Ferron purchased the White Cross Drug Store and began managing two drug stores. It was started in 1919 by J.W. Woodard and Paul Locke and with three employees was located just to the west of the post office on the southwest corner of Fremont and 2nd Street in the Griffith Building (the Golden Nugget today). It had numerous ownership changes in the short period prior to Ferron purchasing it. In 1921 Ferron moved it into larger quarters slightly to the east at the southeast corner of Fremont and Second.

Photo circa 1930 of the White Cross Drug store on the southeast corner of Fremont and 2nd Streets
UNLV Libraries, Special Collections; Ferron-Bracken Photo Collection (0001 0023)

The Ferron's enjoyed long road trips to California -- to visit Long Beach, San Francisco, Carmel and partake in fishing adventures in the High Sierras. They also explored Arizona by car with Walter Bracken and his wife. The family went on an extended road trip in 1926 to Zion, Bryce and Grand Canyons followed by the Lehman Caves, Ely, Reno, Carson City, Lake Tahoe, Yosemite, and Los Angeles. In 1927 they headed to the Reno Exposition, traveling through Beatty, Bishop, Mono Lake, and Carson City. William was partial to camping, golfing and fishing.

In 1924 William hired E.W. Griffith to build a 25 by 85-foot building on Fremont which he leased out to the Oasis Confectionary store (he would sell it to the Las Vegas Cleaning Works in early 1929). In 1925 Ferron became president of the newly formed Las Vegas Businessmen's Association.

William's parents had moved from Utah in 1922 to spend their final years in retirement in the Los Angeles area. His mother Helene passed away in 1928 after a long illness. His father Augustus would die just six weeks later.

In March of 1929 William became president of the Las Vegas Planning Commission. Six months later in September a new post office building opened on Carson between First and Second Streets. The new Sullivan Building completed next door would lease storefronts to businesses. William rented space in the building in October to open his third local pharmacy which he called the "Post Office Drug Store".

October 4, 1929, Las Vegas Review Journal ad

At about the same time, another building (called the Professional Building) was opening on the south side of Fremont and east of Fourth Street, almost directly across from Ferron's home. Businesses were slowly working their way east down Fremont Street as the city grew. Ferron leased space in the new building and established his "Professional Drug Store" in October of 1929. With these two almost simultaneous additions William was now associated with four pharmacies in close vicinity to each other in the downtown Las Vegas area. Ferron shared ownership in all four businesses with Dr. Roy Martin. In 1930 they reorganized and remodeled the interior of their Las Vegas Pharmacy at Fremont and 1st. They put in new modern refrigeration equipment and extended their Sunday hours of operation. After William experienced a possible case of smallpox in 1930, he decided to no longer sport a mustache.

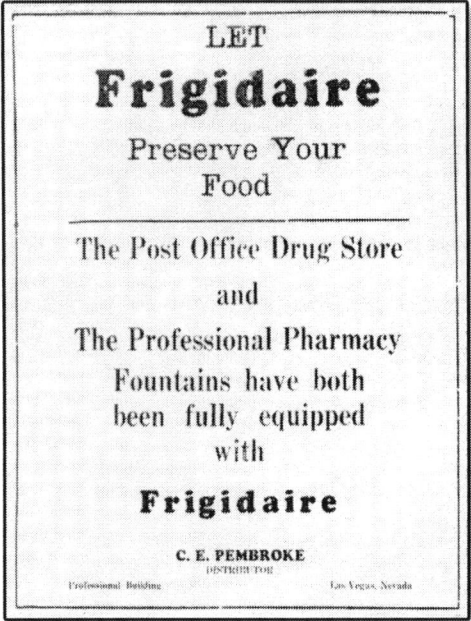

October 5, 1929, Las Vegas Age ad for two of Ferron's drug stores

May 13, 1932, Las Vegas Age ad for summer products being sold at all four of his locations

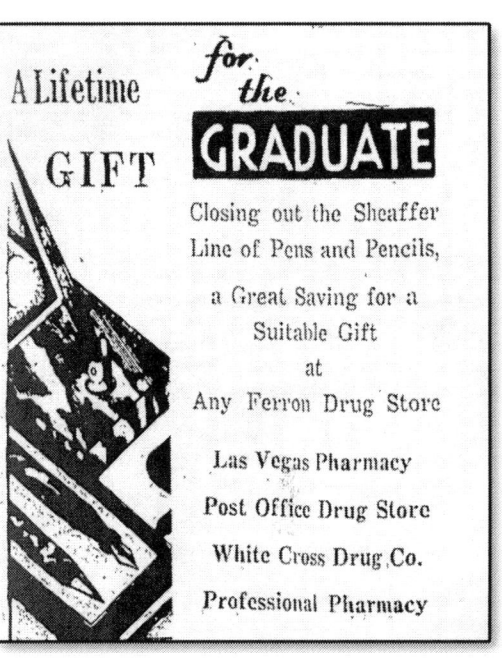

May 29, 1933, Las Vegas Review Journal ad

Dr. Martin wanted to focus his attention on his growing hospital facilities, so in March of 1931 he sold all his interests in the drug stores to William who then became sole proprietor.

With the Great Depression in full swing in 1931, William became chairman of the Community Relief Fund and helped raise $1000 over six months. In June of 1933 he joined the Nevada State Pharmacy Board and would be its distinguished president for an incredible sixteen years.

In July of 1933 the Ferron family headed to Chicago for the Century of Progress Exposition. On their way home they travelled through Canada to the West Coast and then down to Fresno before returning to Las Vegas. In 1934 William had a successful run as Clark County Director of Depression-era projects. After the Boulder Dam was completed, Ferron shed two of his pharmacies, the Professional Pharmacy and the Post Office Drug Store (which he sold in February of 1935 to a group of local men). He had taken on a partner who apparently was stealing from the till.

Undated photo circa late 1930's of Ruth Ferron
UNLV Libraries, Special Collections;
Dokter Photo Collection (0012 0103)

By the time William found out, the pharmacies were near bankruptcy. His partner fled without prosecution and William had to borrow funds to stay afloat. Shedding the two newer locations was a necessity to raise funds and streamline. His finances eventually stabilized.

In 1935 Ferron was reelected president of the Mutual Building and Loan Association and that summer the family vacationed in San Diego and Laguna Beach.

We jump ahead to 1941 when William became president of the new Bank of Nevada which had offices in Las Vegas and Boulder City. He also bought the "Nevada Drug Store" in Boulder City. In 1942 the family moved into a new home on So. 5th Place. By this time the Ferron's were spending ten months a year in Las Vegas with two summer months in Laguna Beach, California where they owned a home. In September William started building a structure on the northeast corner of Fremont and 4th (now Denny's in the Neonopolis complex) where he had razed his old residence that he purchased from the Park family decades earlier. It would house three stores, one of which would be a restaurant. A second adjacent building on North 4th Street would follow in early 1948. It would contain two warehouses and four store fronts, one of which was a bakery.

Undated photo circa 1960 of Ted Brandt and William Ferron
UNLV Libraries, Special Collections;
Ferron Manuscript Collection (MS-00061)

In October of 1948 Ferron took on a partner, Ted Brandt, in his White Cross Drug Store at Fremont and 2nd Streets. Brandt had been living in Boulder City and managing Ferron's store there as a partner. When Ferron sold the store, Brandt moved to Las Vegas to partner in the White Cross store with William. In 1948 they adopted the store motto "The place to go for the brands you know".

In 1952 William and Ruth joined other Rotarians and their wives on a world-wide trip. In 1954 the Las Vegas Pharmacy at Fremont and 1st was forced to close when the Thomas Building was sold to be razed for a new casino.

In February of 1954 the Ferron's took a 55-day cruise to South America. William was anxious to visit his brother Robert who was still a mining engineer and living at the time in Lima, Peru. In September of 1956, Ferron and Brandt opened a second White Cross Drug Store at what is now 1700 Las Vegas Blvd. South in an attempt to capture the growing "Strip" trade. (It remained an important community resource until 2012 when it became a food market and in 2020 the property was sold.)

The Ferron's again travelled the world in 1958, spending a full month in Africa. A trip to the Orient would follow in 1960 and then a visit to Alaska in 1961.

December 3, 1955 Las Vegas Review Journal photo

Newspaper ad circa 1961 for the
White Cross Drug Store's two locations

In 1964 a company purchased the entire frontage of south Fremont Street between 2nd and 3rd Streets to build the Four Queens Hotel and Casino. Stores were forced to close. Ferron and Brandt relocated their pharmacy to 402 Fremont Street in Ferron's building and called their new store the White Cross Rexall Drug Store.

A nighttime photo circa 1965 of the White Cross Drug Store
at the northeast corner of Fremont and 4th Streets
UNLV Libraries, Special Collections; Manis Photo Collection (0100 1836)

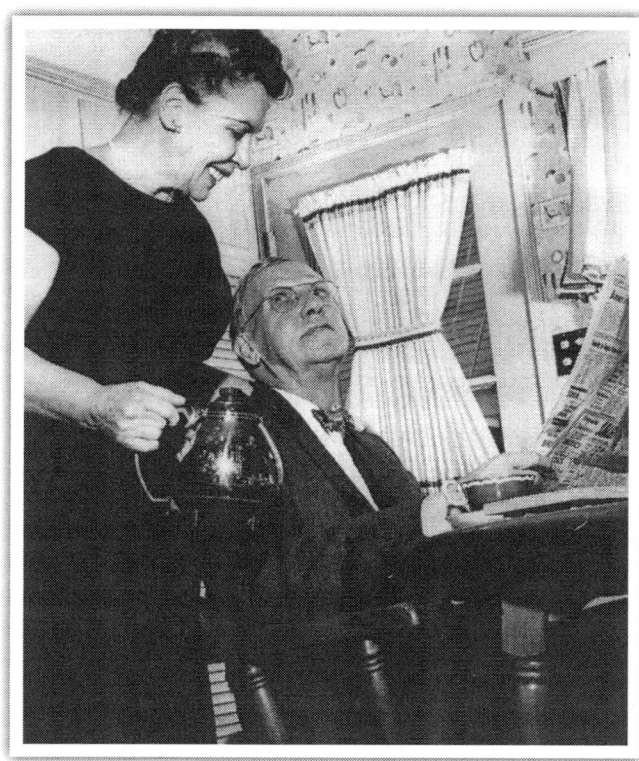

An undated photo circa 1963 of
Ruth and William Ferron at home
Courtesy of the Nevada State Museum, Las Vegas

By now Ferron was working just part-time with Brandt handling the day-to-day operations. William passed away on January 5, 1965, at Sunrise Hospital at age 77. He died from congestive heart failure after a series of strokes. William was buried at the Las Vegas Palm Downtown Cemetery. He and wife Ruth had six grandchildren from daughters Barbara and Shirley. The ladies would eventually sell their inherited stake in the pharmacies to Brandt's widow.

William belonged to the Elks, Shriners, Masons, and was a charter Rotary Club member. Ruth Ferron died on November 15, 1990, at age 97 and was buried next to William. She had been president of the local ladies Mesquite Club from 1922 to 1923 and belonged to the "Tuesday Bridge Club" for 60 years. She was very active in the Las Vegas community and had belonged to many local organizations.

An elementary school was named for William Ferron in 1970. Daughter Barbara passed away in 1994 at age 76 in Berkley, California. Daughter Shirley died in 2013 in Las Vegas at age 93.

William was not only a mayor of Las Vegas, but was also the longest serving pharmacist in the city's history. He was a major booster of the city's image. William Ferron definitely left his mark on Las Vegas.

A 1939 UCLA yearbook
photo of Barbara Ferron
Ancestry.org

A 1940 UCLA yearbook
photo of Shirley Ferron
Ancestry.org

Chapter 17
Scammers, Schemers and Dreamers

Over the last forty years, Las Vegas has witnessed many spectacular proposed projects come and go. Resorts, hotels, shopping centers, business districts, and entertainment venues were announced with great fanfare and often with the backing of celebrities in the sports and the entertainment world only never to come to fruition. It was not much different about 100 years ago when outsiders surfaced in Las Vegas with exciting proposals to build resort hotels or massive housing tracts. In this chapter, many of these "air projects" as they have been nicknamed will be discussed. They sounded amazing to residents, perhaps too amazing. Most faded away after much hype. We begin with the story of a sensational gold mine just outside of Las Vegas from over a century ago. From there, the saga blends into real estate investments and housing developments, including hotels and resorts. Some of the players were interesting characters who surfaced in more than one role.

PART I -- PAUL WATELET AND HIS GOLD MINE

As Las Vegas established itself as a railroad town in 1905, it was only natural for its residents to pay close attention to developments in the not so far away mining districts of Eldorado Canyon, Searchlight, Goldfield, Bullfrog, and Rhyolite. Even though most believed Las Vegas' mountainous areas lacked promising precious metal reserves, folks eagerly followed general mining news that was published in virtually every issue of the Las Vegas Age and Las Vegas Times newspapers. Those prospering mining districts also served as excellent markets for surplus goods being sold in the young town of Las Vegas.

One day in late 1905 when a stranger with a heavy foreign accent showed up in town to buy food and mining supplies for his supposed new gold mining venture about 8 miles southeast of town, the ears of residents perked up with excitement. Who was this man? Did he indeed find gold so close to town?

The man's name was Paul Watelet (pronounced "What-let"). He was a stranger to all in town and at first was pretty secretive about his mining claim. No one knew who he really was and if his rumored find was genuine. Before getting to his gold mine story, I can share Watelet's background thanks to today's internet newspaper search capabilities. Something that was not available to the local town folks back in the early 1900's. If they only knew...

Paul Watelet was born in Belgium in January of 1858. In the1880's Belgium was continuing to experience political and economic turmoil and violence. Western Canada, with a growing coal mining industry needed to support steam cruisers, began a recruiting program in Belgium to attract miners to work on Vancouver Island. Watelet acted

A 1913 photo of Paul Watelet
UNLV Libraries, Special Collections

as an agent for Canada in Belgium to attract such experienced workers. They were promised good wages and working conditions, which unfortunately did not prove to be true. Not all found employment and their supposed pay had been misrepresented. In the late 1880's, Canada also began offering 64 hectares of free quality farming land to attract experienced Belgian farmers. It is likely that the offer resulted in Watelet's decision to leave Belgium. He arrived in British Columbia, Canada around 1888 and became a naturalized U.S. citizen in May of 1891. In 1892 he was living in Victoria, Canada and working as a mining engineer. He set up a coal mining operation (with three partners from New York) on the 900-acre Tumbo Island. He had an office in Victoria and purchased supplies and equipment in Seattle. He claimed his ore was of superior quality.

By 1896 he was working several claims along Maus Creek in Fort Steel, Canada (about 30 miles east of Kootenay and 230 miles east of Vancouver) with two Japanese prospectors. In early 1898 Watelet was in San Francisco trying to convince capitalists from Indianapolis to buy his mining interests. He was co-owner and superintendent of the "Golden Crown Mine". The 1900 U.S. Census showed Watelet living in Flatcreek, Washington and working as a miner, owning his own house.

In late 1902 Paul was organizing the "Leopold Mining Company" with two partners in Stevens County, Washington (in the northeast corner of the state and about 75 miles from Kootenay, Canada). Watelet took up residence in the swanky Hotel Spokane in early 1903. He mingled with Spokane's most distinguished citizens who were fascinated with his foreign accent and thought he may be of royal European ancestry. Paul was known to "cut a dash in Spokane high society".

In mid-May of 1903 the hotel noticed that Watelet had disappeared, abandoning his luggage in his room. He left Spokane just days before the filing of a lawsuit against him for fraudulently obtaining $4,000 from John Carnahan, an oil, steel and iron magnate from Ohio. Paul claimed he found a rich vein of ore in Stevens County and convinced Carnahan to invest. Carnahan actually came to inspect the claim and found it did not exist. Watelet had also convinced a friend, Ernest Leverson (an owner of timberlands in British Columbia), to invest $1,200. It turned out that Watelet had an outstanding British Columbia warrant on him for embezzling $450 from his own mining company. The press referred to him as "Count Watelet" and mentioned that he was out on a $2000 bond.

Paul Watelet was caught by a detective on an eastbound Canadian train in late May of

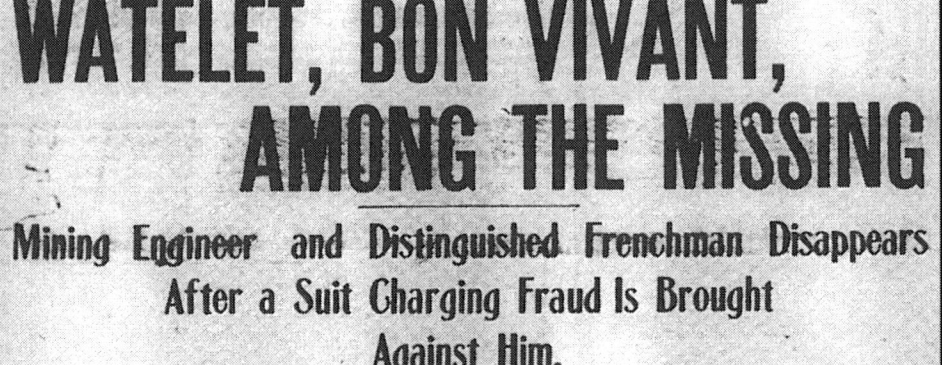

Headline in a May 1903 Spokane newspaper

1903 and detained by instructions of the Vancouver Chief of Police. He was taken to the Ashcroft, British Columbia jail to await transfer back to Vancouver to stand charges. His friend Leverson went to Ashcroft and was able to get his $1200 returned. Watelet had $2000 on him at the time of his arrest. Charges were dropped and he was released from custody, only to be rearrested immediately to await extradition to Spokane. Officials in Spokane were already trying to garnish bank funds belonging to "the dapper French mining engineer" (his Belgian accent was often confused with a French one).

While awaiting transfer, Watelet slept in the Ashcroft jail. With an escort, he was able to dine at a local hotel. He bought his guards cigars and meals with wine. He was called a "smooth worker". Local officials said if he fought extradition he would be charged with bringing stolen money into Canada, a crime that carried up to a seven year sentence.

In early June of 1903 Watelet was moved to a Vancouver jail cell where he would have less freedom. Other victims were expected to surface and he was also charged with not repaying a six-year-old $600 I.O.U.. Mr. Carnahan arrived from Mexico to confront Watelet face to face. Paul finally arrived in Spokane in mid-June. The local paper said the "Princely-looking Watelet looked well and dapper". Bail was set at $4000. Friends of Watelet were unable to come up with his bail. The case against Paul stalled when Carnahan came down with appendicitis in Seattle.

The "bon vivant Watelet" pleaded not guilty of "obtaining money under fraudulent misrepresentations" in early July. As the charges against him were read, the "swell little Frenchman never winced". Jury selection in Colville, Washington began a few weeks later and the press reported that Watelet "walked into the courtroom like he was entering a ballroom function; suave and self-contained". Paul was accompanied by three attorneys and two staunch friends.

Watelet's defense was that the $4,000 came from an Ohio bank and not directly from Mr. Carnahan. His attorney's claimed that if any crime was committed, it was one that should be tried in Ohio. It worked. Charges were dropped. However, the sheriff from Canton, Ohio requested Watelet be held for transfer to Ohio to stand trial. Surprisingly Washington Governor McBride refused to sign the extradition papers, saying only that he believed the witnesses against Watelet did not act in good faith. Needless to say, most were shocked. The Governor was heavily criticized. Paul was once again released.

Article from the July 8, 1903, Spokane Press

Article from the August 13, 1903, Spokane press

In mid-August a "radiant Watelet" said to the press "this is the eighth time I have been arrested in this state and in British Columbia and every time I have been cleared and gone free". He immediately returned to the Hotel Spokane after his near three-month ordeal. In his broken English he said, "I was not ze social Pope of Spokane". After taking a short vacation, he planned to live in Seattle. By the end of 1903 Paul disappeared again and was believed to be living in Mexico in 1904. At that time a detective agency was again looking for him after he fled with $1000 from a mining investment deal that went sour. Also Mr. Carnhan was still trying to find him to have him face charges in Ohio.

In 1905 Watelet was associated with two mines in California and is believed to have ties to the Pacific Coast Gypsum Co. which had offices in San Francisco and a mill in Tacoma, Washington.

Now that we know a lot about Watelet's shady background we can get to his Las Vegas connection. In October of 1905 Paul is managing a gypsum mining operation about ten miles east of the new town of Las Vegas. How he wound up there is not known. He intended to search for gold in the area as well. Paul established a small camp about two miles to the east of the gypsum site where he found water and shade trees. He supervised four Belgian workers and planned to send gypsum to Los Angeles and San Francisco. Nearby young Las Vegas became his go-to destination to pick up tools, supplies and food.

Article from the Dec. 24, 1903 Missoulian, Montana newspaper.

Photos of Alexina and Naomi in the July 10, 1908 Oakland Tribune. They had just returned from a ten-month tour of Europe

In February of 1906 Watelet claimed to have 12 men starting a tunnel to hunt for gold. He set up a small office at Hotel Nevada so he could communicate by telegram with company people in California. The April 1906 destructive San Francisco earthquake disrupted his communications and there was a delay in his placing an order for two train carloads of machinery. In May of 1906 Paul married Naomi Dunning in Alameda County in California. Naomi was 37 years old and had a daughter by the name of Alexina from a prior marriage.

By early summer of 1906, Watelet placed his gypsum operation on hold as he focused his attention on his gold mine that then had 12 men at work. Between 1907 and 1911 work was proceeding on his "promising" gold mine. Paul made numerous trips to town for supplies and also made trips to California to visit his wife and stepdaughter. He would often stay in California for months on end. His wife Naomi lived in Oakland and had been the proprietor of the Touraine Hotel in San Francisco. When it was heavily damaged in the big 1906 earthquake, she retired. Naomi died in June of 1910 after a brief illness. Paul returned to handle her affairs.

Undated photo of the entrance of Watelet's mine
UNLV Libraries, Special Collections

A photo circa 1908 of four men at the mining camp
UNLV Libraries, Special Collections

A photo circa 1909 of Watelet's mining camp
UNLV Libraries, Special Collections

Undated photo of Frenchman Mountain
UNLV Libraries, Special Collections

Watelet's at-first secret gold mine was located near the base of a mountain east of town. When he appeared in Las Vegas, folks (as usual) had a hard time understanding his broken English, mistaking his Belgian accent as being French. Thus, they gossiped about the "Frenchman's Mine" and that is how today's Frenchman Mountain got its name.

Paul was not alone in his gold mining venture. A medical doctor from Berkeley, California by the name of George Washington Hillegass put up the money to organize the Southern Nevada Gold Mining Company (SNGM Co.) in 1909. Dr. Hillegass was the president of the company and Watelet was his partner and the mine's manager. SNGM Co.'s operation outside of town was believed to be the first gold claim close to Las Vegas. Others had tried to find gold but lacked the capital investment needed. This operation was different -- Paul was a mining engineer and Dr. Hillegass was able to find backers. They claimed to have raised

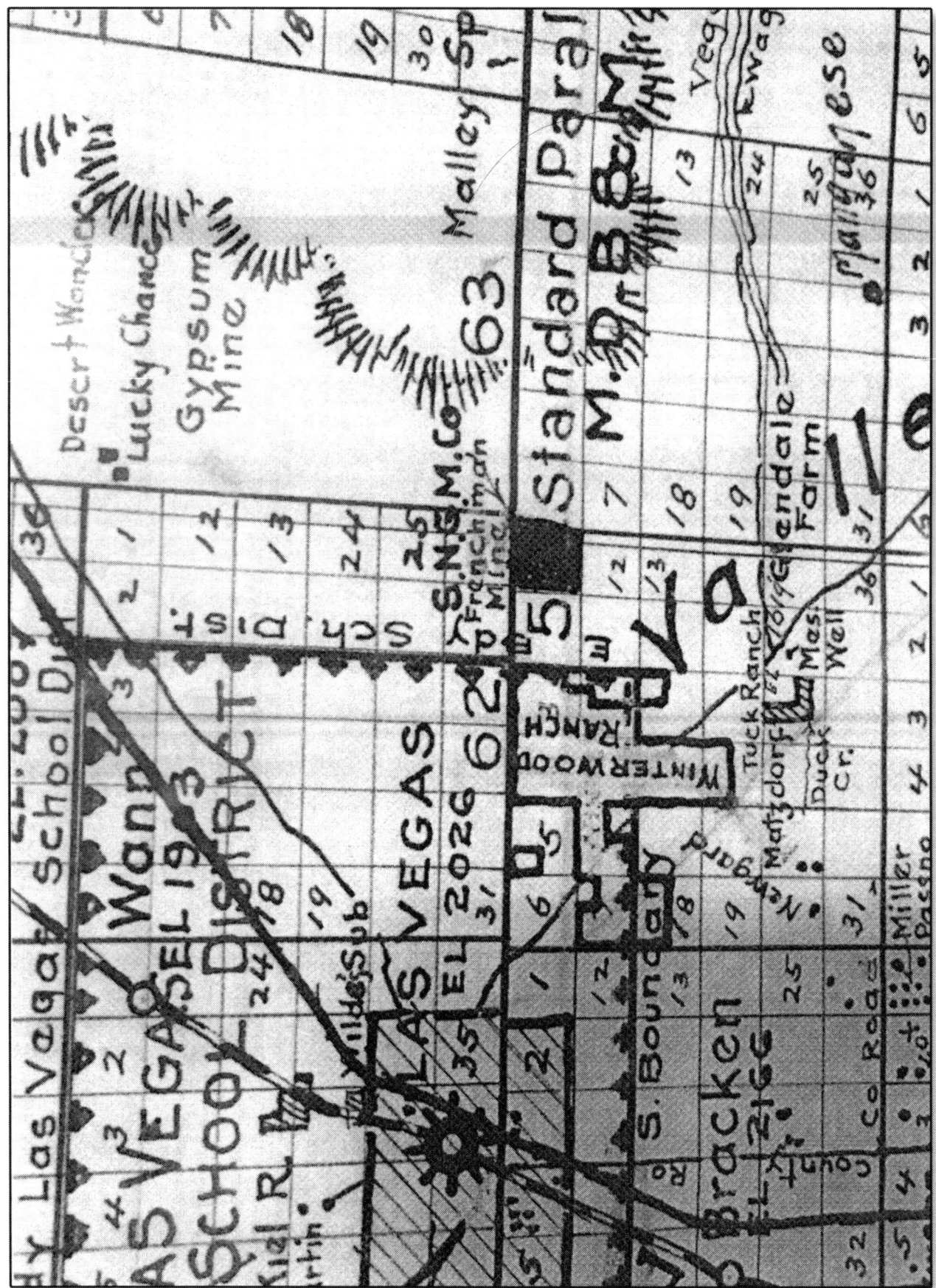

Map showing location of the mine (black square) with the Winterwood Ranch off to its west
Clark County Museum map collection

$100,000 from investors. SNGM Co. began buying up large sections of empty desert to the west of their mine. In May of 1911, SNGM Co. sold over 5000 of their acres to William J. Latchford of California. Latchford was a manufacturer of glass bottles in Los Angeles. He had land and mining interests and was President of the Clark County Land Company. He called his land purchase from SNGM Co. the "Winterwood Ranch". Latchford made plans to drill an artesian well and plant up to 340 acres in grains by the end of 1911. By early 1912 his Winterwood Ranch had ample water.

In February of 1912, Watelet showed up in town and talked of finding a rich vein of gold some 800 feet into his mine. Word of the "Frenchman's big gold strike" was met at first with some skepticism. But after over six years of hard work, Paul was able to show off chunks of his sparkling ore to the locals. (People later on believed the ore Watelet produced came from elsewhere.)

Now needing money to build a mill and formal campgrounds, Dr. Hillegass and Paul Watelet sold 49% of their SNGM Co. for $375,000 to two companies -- the Clark County Land Co. and the Winterwood Land Co., both controlled by William Latchford and his three partners (John Winters, Charles Palmer and John Prophet). Watelet was kept on as manager and paid in stock. Plans were started to build a large milling plant by the mine. Latchford had thoughts of starting a new town to be called Winterwood on his adjacent ranch land. In time he believed it could rival Las Vegas.

Undated photo showing Paul Watelet in white in the center

Paul now had the capital to complete a 2400-foot-long tunnel and would spend $24,000 on a ventilation system. In March of 1912 he gave an interview to the Las Vegas Age during which he mentioned that his mine had a potential value of $500,000 and might lead to two new nearby towns to be called Hillegass and Winterwood. Despite his obvious excitement, he said he did not really want publicity.

Watelet started construction of a significant mining camp that would include an office, cottages, bunk houses for workers, and a commissary. By April the tunnel was completed. In October enough lumber was brought to the mine for the building of some 30 small cottages, each to house two workers. Fifty workers would be needed with up to 200 total once a mill was operating. Water was found at the camp, enough for the mine's needs. By early 1913 twenty-five men were at work and Watelet

1913 photo of visitors at the mine. From left to right are a miner and his wife, Will Beckley, Leva Beckley, Paul Watelet, and Jake Beckley.
UNLV Libraries, Special Collections

allowed people from Las Vegas to visit. Folks seized the opportunity and made it weekend entertainment. They posed for pictures and were impressed by what Paul was accomplishing.

Undated photo of visitors from Las Vegas at the Frenchman mine
UNLV Libraries, Special Collections

Undated photo of structure at the camp of the Frenchman mine
UNLV Libraries, Special Collections

In February of 1913 Watelet made plans to ship 210 pounds of ore (20 sacks) by Parcel Post to Sacramento for testing. This mode of transportation was new and was brought to the attention of citizens throughout Nevada. (Years later, it could not be confirmed that the sacks were ever really sent.)

In July 1913 Paul took a trip to Paris and Brussels (his home town) to rest and visit family. He was to be gone for some three months during which time the mill would near completion. At the same time, Dr. Hillegass announced his engagement to Emma Gloor of Oakland. Work went forward at the mine at a brisk pace. Machinery arrived and more workers were hired. It was rumored that the gold (found in a mix of galena and black quartzite) could bring some $30 per ton of ore.

Undated Las Vegas Age photo of the mill at the mine

The mill neared final completion in October of 1913. It was estimated that it could crush about 140 tons of ore per day yielding between $20 and $30 worth of gold per ton. Meanwhile, partner Latchford's nearby Winterwood Ranch was producing fruits and vegetables for the mine's workers. The makeshift road from the mine to Las Vegas went through Latchford's Winterwood Ranch and was in poor shape which made it difficult to transport equipment and supplies (lumber, brick, steam boilers, and needed staples). Thus, Latchford proposed the grading of a proper road to be named Winterwood Boulevard that would connect the mine to Las Vegas. He sought the cooperation of the Las Vegas Chamber of Commerce which in those days oversaw roads in the area. The Chamber's road committee seemed agreeable. Winterwood Blvd. would also help mine workers get to and from town along with produce from the ranch. Dr. Hillegass offered $1000 towards the road from the SNGM Co. and Latchford would match it. Latchford pledged to also seek donations from adjacent landowners. Delays in the road occurred when the county had to acquire right-of-way deeds. In the meantime, volunteers began some grading near the mine. The first few miles were getting underway but the work soon stalled.

Watelet had yet to return from Belgium due to his mother's unexpected illness. He sent word to Dr. Hillegass and Latchford that after he returned and got the mill up and running, he wanted to retire. He was about 55 years old.

By early 1914 it was reported that one mill was functioning at the mine and that there were plans for up to three more to be built. Paul Watelet was said to be in Canada. Dr. Hillegass visited the mine and announced he might grade the road to town at his own expense.

Latchford and his partners decided to sell a portion of their Winterwood Ranch to a syndicate of Japanese investors for $100,000 in late January of 1914. It had been sitting fairly inactive for about two years and only 600 acres had been leveled. With California having restrictive land ownership laws at that time, the Japanese gentlemen looked to Nevada to buy land to grow cotton and cantaloupes.

By March, the mill at the gold mine supposedly had doubled its capacity to process ore. It is doubtful that Paul Watelet ever returned to his mine. It was thought that he had returned to Belgium sometime in 1914 to help his sister with her silk factory. It has been written that he may have been killed while protecting his sister's mill during World War I by advancing German armies making their way through Belgium. Many different versions have been told, but none were ever confirmed.

With Watelet back in Europe, Dr. Hillegass began to lose interest in the mine's operation. Maybe because it was not really producing any true gold and he had profited as much as he could before people realized there was really no gold in the ore. He and Watelet were successful in getting investors to buy shares in their operation and made money on large land sales as well. Was there ever any gold? Probably not. Was it all a scam to make it look very real so they could con investors for big bucks? Perhaps.

Dr. Hillegass was a well-educated, successful Berkeley physician who also had offices in Oakland and San Francisco. Just like Watelet did in Spokane years earlier, one day in 1913 Dr. Hillegass plain old disappeared without a trace. He was not to be heard from again. Nobody knows why. Years later, in February of 1927 it was learned that he had died in March of 1925 at age 59 in a Utica, New York hospital and was buried in a pauper's graveyard when nobody claimed his body. When his family found out that his remains had been identified, they had him returned to Oakland for burial in 1927. Claims against his $150,000 estate left little for his heirs to inherit. Information later came out that in 1922 he was spotted in Philadelphia and was broke and unkempt. Also, in early 1925 he had been picked up for vagrancy in New York. Why this happened to a successful doctor and businessman remains a mystery. Newspapers in California reported that he had been involved with numerous failed mining operations. There is no evidence that he ever did marry. In the end, his estate's final value was placed at less than $10,000.

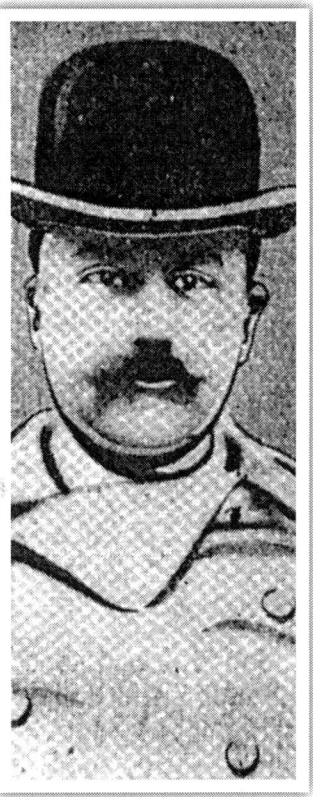

February 15, 1927, Oakland Tribune newspaper photo of what Hillegass looked like

With both Watelet and Hillegass out of the picture, the mining operation outside of Las Vegas slowly faded away. Investors lost their money as the mine never produced any known gold. Some of the structures that had been built were either sold, moved or stolen. The entrance to the mine was boarded up.

Undated photo of remnants of the mine's entrance
UNLV Libraries, Special Collections

The 1912-1914 Nevada Bureau of Mines and Geology Las Vegas District File indicated that the SNGM Co. operation included a 300 ton per day cyanide plant. No ore had been processed in the region. The mill was probably constructed to con people into investing. Ruins of a mill did show up on a topographical map years later. In 1930 the U.S. Department of the Interior classified the mine and land around it as "abandoned". It was most likely all a big scheme that sadly convinced investors, the towns folk and local newspaper that it was genuine and would benefit the future of Las Vegas.

PART II -- WINTERWOOD RANCH HISTORY AND LAND DEVELOPMENTS

In 1915 William Latchford (now a director of a California fruit packing company called the San Fernando Lemon Association) and his partners were still in control of roughly 4000 acres of the Winterwood Ranch with the Japanese men farming the rest of the acreage. They were growing peas, turnips, and many other vegetables that were supplying the Union Pacific's dining cars. In November of 1915 Latchford and his partners sold their Winterwood Ranch to Lycurgus Lindsay and Associates of Los Angeles. The Japanese syndicate then traded their acreage to Lindsay for 115 acres of orange orchards near Bloomington, California. As the new primary owner of the over 5,000-acre Winterwood Ranch, Lindsay announced plans to plant 1000 acres in alfalfa.

Photo of Lycurgus Lindsay circa 1925
Ancestry.org

Lycurgus Lindsay (often misspelled in the newspapers as Lindsey) was a married 56-year-old wealthy investor who in earlier years made his money from flour mills, cattle ranching and copper mining in Mexico. He was often referred to in the papers as "the cattle king of California and Mexico". In June of 1916 Lindsay added the Sund Tract of land to his portfolio in Clark County. He bought it from Judge William Thomas and Dr. Roy Martin who had purchased it from Charles Sund in October 1914. It had a strong functioning artesian well. Lycurgus was the director of the Los Angeles Trust Company.

Undated photo with an unidentified man posing at the artesian well on the Sund Tract
UNLV Libraries, Special Collections

Photo circa 1910 of the building in Los Angeles that housed the Los Angeles Trust Company

By 1920 cotton was being grown on acreage within portions of the Sund and Winterwood tracts. You may recall that the first airplane to land in Las Vegas arrived on May 7, 1920, from Blythe, California with Jake Beckley aboard. What is not well known is that it first landed in error on the nearby Winterwood Ranch which the pilot mistook for Las Vegas (at the time the town had no marked landing field).

In June of 1922 Lycurgus Lindsay announced plans to drill two new wells on his Winterwood Ranch. In June 1923 he was prepared to plant 3000 acres in alfalfa. In 1924 Lindsay was running the Pacific-Southwest Trust in Pasadena, California.

Lycurgus Lindsay and his associates decided to sell their 5,800-acre Winterwood Ranch and 640 acre Sund Tract to 54 year-old T.J. (Thomas Jefferson) Lawrence and his "Lawrence & Co." partners for $500,000 in January of 1927. The new owners at first wanted the Winterwood land for cultivation and within a year had 240 acres in wheat. For the Sund land they envisioned a large housing development that would have a central plaza and business district. They also proposed a large lake and a community pool. Trees and plants would line the streets. Lawrence began work on grading the land the very next month. He was a well-known and respected California developer of many large projects consisting of homes and golf courses.

A 1920's photo of the building in Pasadena, California that was home to the Pacific Southwest Trust

A 1925 photo of the headquarters for T. J. Lawrence Co. at 6th and Hope Streets in Los Angeles. The company was organized in 1923

A September 1, 1923, Los Angeles Evening Post-Record ad for a large T. J. Lawrence land development in the heart of Los Angeles

Photo of T.J. Lawrence in the Feb. 25, 1922, issue of the Los Angeles Evening Express

It was not until February of 1929 that Lawrence showed up in Las Vegas. He released his formal housing development proposal and it was followed by a flurry of activity. His 200-acre subdivision on his Sund Tract would be called the Artesian (or sometimes just "Artesia") Park Estates. It was not that far from Downtown Las Vegas, perhaps a mile or two to the southwest. He chose Frank Riley to be his "man on the ground". Riley said that $15,000 in road equipment would be brought in from California and work would first begin with the central lake. The lake would be followed by the grading and oiling of roads. At the same time, Lawrence announced plans for the

Ad in the March 6, 1929, Las Vegas Review Journal announcing the upcoming Artesian Park Estates

Winterwood Ranch. He was anxious to build an airport for use by Western Air Express and would negotiate to build a smaller temporary airport near the Boulder Dam site. Lawrence also envisioned farming and ranching on the Winterwood Ranch along with a creamery.

Main headline of the March 14, 1929, Las Vegas Age

Lawrence and Riley began lining up Las Vegas real estate brokers to help sell lots in the Artesian Park Estates. They planned to bring in potential buyers from California in April to coincide with the opening of a rodeo near the dam project.

Lawrence ran this ad in the March 23, 1929, Santa Ana Register in California to attract interest in his Las Vegas development

Ad run by Lawrence in the March 23, 1929, Las Vegas Age to create excitement about the future of Las Vegas

Two oil tankers arrived in April and three miles of internal roads were graded. Lawrence's development would have artistic homes with red tile roofs, wide streets, six playgrounds, a central business plaza, and race restrictions. Lawrence envisioned "cascading artesian water through the streets in the hot summer months for cooling". He did have some critics who claimed he was nothing more than a very creative salesman.

Screenshot photo of Lawrence's headquarters on Fremont St. in Las Vegas. Snapped from film footage shown in Part III of the documentary "The City of Las Vegas".
Courtesy of the City of Las Vegas

Potential investors were brought in by train. They received breakfast at the depot while live orchestra music played. Then they were transported to the dam area for a tour of the canyon by Lawrence himself. A metallurgist gave a speech about mining and the Las Vegas Valley. The guests were then shuffled over to the Sund Tract to see the area where his Artesian Park Estates would be developed. Finally, all received a fine dinner at Lawrence's office which he established on Fremont Street (on the north side between 2nd and 3rd Streets) which was followed by band music. Quite an impressive and interesting day for his visitors, capitalists from Los Angeles and San Francisco! Choice corner lots sold quickly.

Lawrence tasked Riley with bringing in a cameraman to film Las Vegas and its environs for a promotional film which was shown on May 4, 1929. Prizes were awarded to attract attendees. T.J. Lawrence was in control of a massive nine square miles of land in the Las Vegas region.

In May, 1929 another promotional tour was conducted which included a boat ride on the Colorado River. Frank Riley was promoted to vice-president of T.J. Lawrence, Inc. and bids were sought for construction of homes. Lawrence envisioned Las Vegas possibly as another Denver.

Lawrence began running ads in the newspaper and to stimulate lot sales he claimed that prices

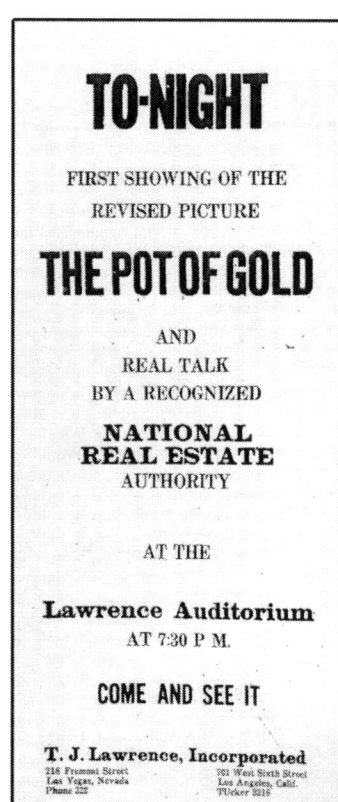

Ad in the May 4, 1929, Las Vegas Review Journal

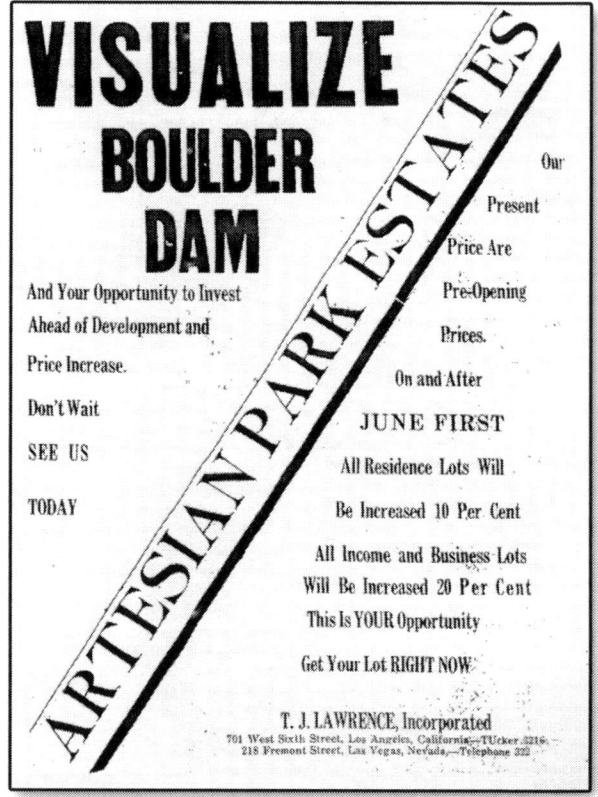

Ad in the May 18, 1929, Las Vegas Review Journal

would soon be going up. In another promotional stunt, he hired Willis Owen (a writer, speaker, and railroad advisor) to tell over the radio the story of Las Vegas, the dam project and the future of the area. Robert Baker, a civil and mining engineer who Lawrence had used for Los Angeles projects, was hired as the new sales manager for the Estates.

Lawrence became upset with the Las Vegas City Commission over the assessed valuation of his housing project. He appeared before the commissioners in August protesting his high tax bill, saying that it assumed project improvements that had not even been started (water, electricity, sidewalks, and sewage). They appeased him and lowered his amount due. In November of 1929 the Boulder Realty Company (which was formed in 1925 by Dr. Roy Martin, Al Minnette and the Ferron brothers) merged with Lawrence's company and moved into his Fremont Street office. Boulder Realty would act as Lawrence's main sales agent in town.

In early 1930 T.J. Lawrence gave his okay to have oil test wells drilled on both his Winterwood Ranch and the Sund Tract. He had just formed a $4 million corporation (Paramount Investments) in Los Angeles to push his interests in the Southwest United States, which included $1 million for his Las Vegas plans.

By the end of the summer in 1930 local real estate brokers were busy reserving lots for clients and construction of the large lake was underway. September saw the construction of the first 25 homes in the Artesian Park Estates with 25 more to soon follow. The Boulder Realty sales office was downsized in November and moved to 11 Fremont Street.

Ad in the November 30, 1929,
Las Vegas Review Journal

In January 1931 Lawrence was sued over a $10,000 note he had with Lycurgus Lindsay from May of 1929. Another note (coming due in February) for $300,000 with the Boulder Canyon Land Development Corp. resulted in a second lawsuit when Lawrence failed to live up to his purchase agreements. Things were beginning to unravel for him. Unable to come up with the funds to settle with his creditors, a sheriff's sale was conducted in March of 1931. Auctioned off were 18 tons of hay and subsoiler equipment. Hundreds of lots in his Artesian Park Estates were placed on the tax delinquency list and foreclosure followed. It could not be determined who finished the project, but a later map showed it as being completed. By the 1950's it was known as the McNeil Tract. Even though he died in 1931, Lycurgus Lindsay's estate took back control of the Winterwood Ranch. (T.J. Lawrence would die in July of 1940. His proposed airport on the Winterwood Ranch was never built.)

The history of Winterwood Ranch advances to the summer of 1947 when W. T. Stewart, his many sons, and Earl Leavitt take over the property. They prepared the land at the foot of Sunrise Mountain for cultivation and fencing. Two years later they were ready to plant barley. By February of 1951 there were 13 Stewart family members working the ranch and they were considering using portions to build homes. The family fiercely came out in opposition to a proposal for an adjacent hog farm and dump.

In February 1953 the ranch had some 800 acres in barley, alfalfa, and corn. The Stewart parents, now in their seventies, announced they would be going on a mission to southern states. So the Winterwood Ranch would be broken up in 1954 with the largest portion going to S.J. Lawson who was once President of the Las Vegas Power Company.

The Stewarts and members of the Bunker family sold the remaining Winterwood Ranch acreage in June of 1963 for $5 million to Paradise Homes, controlled by land developer Merv Adelson. Some 1600 acres were set aside for a public 18-hole golf course called Desert Rose to the south. Plans were announced for the building of 4,500 homes along with stores, churches and schools. It was a $100 million project that involved multiple builders. By October of 1963 homes were being built and the golf course project was set at 444 acres. Work on the golf course started in March of 1964. Today the Winterwood Ranch region is a large residential area that has tributes to its earlier heritage -- a Winterwood Boulevard and a large Winterwood HOA. At its peak Winterwood Ranch ran from Charleston to Sahara (north to south) and from Pecos to the Las Vegas Wash (west to east).

Next we move into a discussion of impressive hotel proposals.

PART III -- HOTEL AND RESORT PROJECTS

In the beginning days of Las Vegas lodging was an important necessity. Very early arrivals either resided in their own makeshift tents or at the Old Ranch which fell under the control of the railroad. We have seen how Captain Ladd set up the first tent hotel (on Main Street) to house visitors in early 1905. It offered not much more than a few cots which were to be shared. The much larger white canvas tent Hotel Las Vegas followed by "Pop" Squires. It offered a dining room and some privacy. Soon small wooden hotels popped up. The nice Hotel Nevada and Overland Hotel at the corners of Fremont and Main followed. They were more permanent in nature and offered clean rooms, running water, electricity, dining options, bars, barbershops and other needed services. However, they were not in the same league as today's mega-resorts on the Strip. Nonetheless, there were numerous attempts by forward-looking investors ("dreamers") in the 1920's and 1930's to build luxurious hotel resorts in the Las Vegas area that would attract both locals and travelers from afar. Some of those projects would not get past the drawing board state before self-destructing. Others made commendable progress before being abandoned.

The first person to come up with the idea of building a large resort hotel in Las Vegas was Alex Richmond, a wealthy California hotel developer and owner. He was responsible for many impressive hotels in California, including the one in Santa Barbara that was heavily damaged by a 1925 earthquake while the Brackens were guests there. (Over his lifetime he also owned and operated the Barbara Worth Hotel in El Centro, the Planters Hotel in Brawley, the Arlington Hotel in Santa Barbara, and the Arlington Lodge in Lake Arrowhead.)

Richmond (age 59) happened to visit Las Vegas in January of 1926 while on a tour of the potential Black Canyon dam site. He was impressed by what local and state officials had to say about the promising future of the region. In March he announced his intentions to build a top-class tourist hotel in the area that would also attract additional investments. The Las Vegas Age newspaper wrote with enthusiasm about Richmond's plans.

Headline of the March 13, 1926, Las Vegas Age

Richmond asked the Union Pacific Railroad (which bought out its SP - LA- SL Railroad partner) for 100 acres for his project. They agreed but turned down his request that they also provide free water. Walter Bracken, the railroad's town agent, stepped up in support and offered $25,000 to improve the land surrounding the project. Richmond sought to get the backing of local residents by asking that they purchase $50,000 in stock. He pegged his project as having a cost of $500,000.

In the fall of 1926, the Union Pacific offered 90 acres just northeast of town to Richmond. In the early months of 1927, the cost of Richmond's project was varying between $500,000 and $750,000. The city and county approved the transfer of Union Pacific land to Richmond. Room rates for the impressive new hotel would begin at $12 per day. An architect was hired with intentions to have the hotel completed by the end of 1927.

Headline of the February 12, 1927, Las Vegas Age

No work had begun in the fall and the anticipated cost of Richmond's "modern tourist hotel" swelled to $1 million by April of 1927. In late May the Chamber of Commerce agreed to assist in the sale of the $50,000 worth of stock to local residents that Richmond requested. The funds would be held by the Chamber until Richmond could prove to railroad executives that he had secured sufficient funding for the entire project (and then the designated land would be transferred to him). Community members quickly purchased $32,000 in stock as they realized the value of such a project to the city. How could it not be of significant benefit to Las Vegas?

In early July 1927 Richmond announced that design plans were nearly done and that construction would finally begin in August or September. Locals had reached the required $50,000 goal for stock sales. The latest cost associated with the hotel project had dropped to $600,000. The hotel would have a banquet room, convention space, 150 "handsome" rooms, an all-grass golf course, fountains, and a horse riding academy. Its location was to be on the north side of town, between the Arrowhead Trail and the 5th St. Highway.

When Richmond failed to show proof of financial backing, his project seemed doomed. He had already asked for and obtained numerous time extensions from the railroad. In October of 1927, "Pop" Squires (owner and publisher of the Las Vegas Age) ran an editorial in which he cautioned his readers that delays and disappointments associated with such a large project are often to be expected. He still believed the resort would be built. He was too optimistic. Richmond's plans for a resort hotel collapsed. He had unsuccessfully approached 21 bond houses and banking firms seeking financial support. Some of them said his project was "too pioneering" and that "Nevada was not looked upon as an inviting territory for bond underwriting".

An undated photo of Leigh Smith James Hunt in his earlier days
Find A Grave

A newspaper photo of Leigh Hunt in his later years of the early 1930's
Ancestry.org

A competing player, Leigh Hunt (age 72 and originally from Cleveland), had emerged in 1927. He had moved to Las Vegas in 1923 and was a former teacher, college administrator, newspaper owner, land investor, railroad owner, explorer (supposedly the first white man to explore the Nile, coming in contact with "savage tribes"), banker and industrialist. He ran a gold mining company in Korea (owned by the emperor of Japan) and was growing Egyptian cotton in the Sudan. Hunt had sizeable wealth and important connections. He liked that Las Vegas had water, farming and nearby minerals so he chose it as his place for retirement. Hunt believed Las Vegas had a suitable climate for a resort tourist hotel.

In 1927 Hunt had begun discussions with the city's mayor, railroad executives, Walter Bracken and Dr. Martin about how he might attract Cleveland investors. With Richmond's project faltering, the Union Pacific offered him 90 acres south of town. Hunt's proposed "Desert Resort Hotel" would have a pool and tennis courts along with a golf course. He hired an architect to begin design planning.

Little progress was made by Hunt during the summer of 1927 and in October his architect backed out. It appeared that his project would come to a halt before even getting started. However, in early 1928 his Cleveland friends began to show their financial support. They thought the hotel should be located not too far south of town and wanted it to mirror a resort complex they had seen in Palm Springs, California.

With new energy, Hunt revised his plans with a revealed price tag of $500,000. The hotel would have 150 rooms and Hunt would be investing $20,000 of his own money. His architect returned and even invested $10,000. Locals were asked to buy $1,000 block shares of stock and Walter Bracken would seek an investment from the railroad. Hunt set a one-year deadline to reach $150,000 in local stock sales and he would arrange for $400,000 in additional funding. In March, 1928 the Cleveland capitalists asked that the railroad work with the city and county to place a deed for the 90 offered acres in escrow before they would put up their initial guarantee of $50,000 to cover construction of the first phase of the hotel (which might be completed by November).

In April of 1928 the demands of the investors were met and hopefully the first wing of the hotel could have paying guests by January of 1929. Project costs were now at $1 million. The summer of 1928 saw plans advance and final details negotiated. Work would hopefully commence in September. It was hoped that the hotel would be able to accommodate workers and officials tied to the upcoming nearby Boulder Dam project.

Hunt's associates deposited $25,000 in earnest money in August of 1929 at the First State Bank on Fremont Street and the remaining $25,000 was to follow within 60 days. Revised construction costs ballooned to $1.5 million. The central hotel structure was to have 152 guest rooms. Bungalows were to be built for staff along with their own swimming pool. The grounds would now encompass 633 acres with a guest pool, tennis courts, a golf course and a small adjacent airfield.

Early 1930 arrived and the second payment of $25,000 had not been deposited in the bank. Hunt's backers believed the project was too far away from the heart of Las Vegas (close to 2 miles) and unsuccessfully attempted to get their initial deposit returned. When Hunt's best efforts failed to convince the Union Pacific Railroad to invest in his project, he threw in the towel. Just like Richmond's project, Hunt's would also vaporize.

While Richmond's and Hunt's resorts were in developmental stages, there were two additional large hotel projects under consideration -- one outside of town and the other on Fremont Street.

As Leigh Hunt's project was struggling, T. J. Lawrence (who as you may recall was busy with his Winterwood and Sund Tracts since buying them in 1927) was watching. Lawrence was prepared to take on a hotel project with or without the help of the railroad executives. He liked the idea of a large resort hotel but believed he could build it on his Winterwood property to avoid dealing with the railroad's people. His proposed airport could also be developed at the same time along with an adjacent 120-acre golf course. In March of 1929 Lawrence asked the city and railroad to transfer land north of Stewart and between 2nd and 5th Streets to his company. The land had been set aside for a city park. Lawrence wanted to subdivide it for housing so he could raise money for his $1.45 million hotel/airport/golf project on Winterwood. The city balked at his request and with no strong financial backing lined up, Lawrence's dream of his so-called "Desert Ambassador" resort project never came to be.

Another near simultaneous hotel project was to be on Fremont Street. This one was to be by none other than George Wingfield (age 51), the richest man in Nevada. Wingfield made his money in mining, banking, and hotels. By age 30 he was already worth $20 to $30 million. Many were calling him "The King of Nevada".

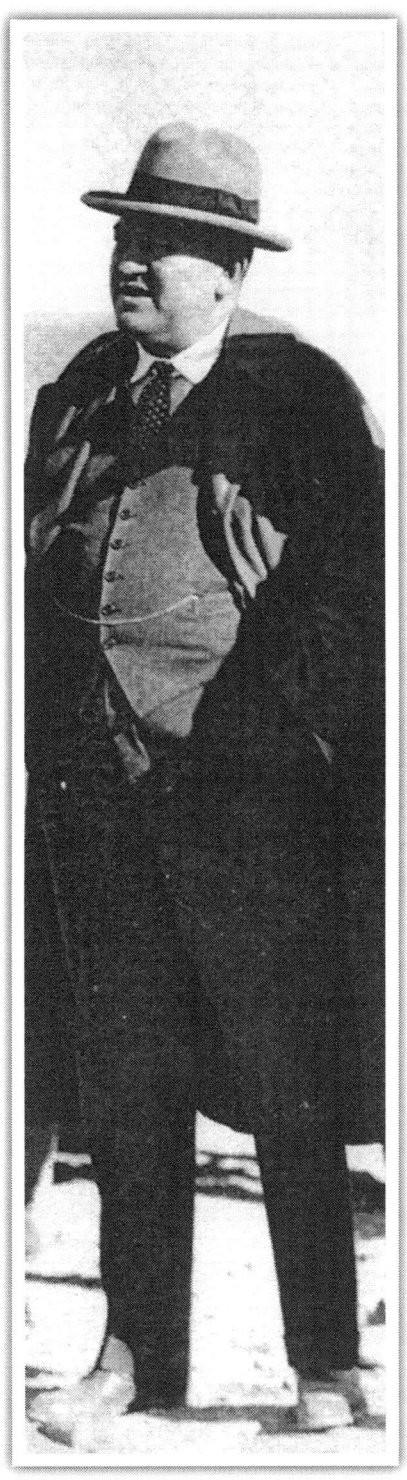

Photo of George Wingfield in 1924
UNLV Libraries, Special Collections;
Fred & Maureen Wilson Photo
Collection (0014 0359)

In December of 1928 Wingfield purchased four lots on the northeast corner of Fremont and 2nd from Dr. Roy Martin for $30,000. The Boulder Dam construction bill had recently been signed and Wingfield was already thinking about its impact on the community. He wanted to build a half-million-dollar first-class hotel on the corner, similar to his two fancy ones in Reno. It would be either 4 or 5 stories in height with a full basement. On the first floor would be the lobby, a coffee shop, a few stores, a dining room and a ballroom for dancing. The hotel would have two wings with a twelve-foot-wide courtyard between them. The second floor would be devoted to office space. Two elevators would be installed along with a modern heating plant. During the summer months cold air would be pumped to all rooms. Every guest room would have its own private bathroom. Wingfield anticipated each floor would cost $100,000 to build.

In January of 1929 Wingfield purchased adjacent footage on Fremont for $15,000 and the Chamber of Commerce was forced to relocate. In February his plans stood at four floors and 150 rooms. The building's foundation would be of sufficient strength to handle the weight of up to three additional floors later on, if desired. Construction might begin in April with completion by January of 1930. All the structures on the lots were cleared off and Wingfield gave his hotel the working name of the "Fremont Hotel". In early April Wingfield changed his mind and wanted his hotel to be five stories tall and asked his engineers for an updated cost estimate. The hotel would have 150 feet of frontage on Fremont and 130 feet on No. 2nd Street. Construction would take seven months. Wingfield was upset with his architect's per room cost projection. In May of 1929 Wingfield and his wife of some 21 years divorced.

George Wingfield continued to reject revised hotel designs as being too costly and plans stalled. In August "Pop" Squires expressed his hope that the project would be brought back to life in the fall. Wingfield lost interest in the whole idea and in mid-September sold the land to Milo Emmerson (age 48), a local businessman, for $75,000. Emmerson wanted to continue with the idea of a hotel on the corner. He sought financial backing from the Reno Securities Company. His hotel would have 120 rooms and be a "Class A" product. He wanted his structure to be fireproof with a steel frame and pegged his construction costs at $275,000. Milo had a 30-day option to follow through on the purchase of the land but let it lapse. He still wanted to build a hotel, but not on Fremont Street. He lost his small down payment. Yet another hotel project bit the dust. (The Great Depression hit George Wingfield and his banks hard by 1932 and he declared bankruptcy in 1935.)

Thus hotel/resort projects by Richmond, Hunt, Lawrence, Wingfield and Emmerson were never completed. There were, however, two significant hotel projects that were actually successfully built in the early 1930's.

The Apache Hotel opened inside the new Boulder Club on the northwest corner of Fremont and 2nd Street. The other, the Meadows Hotel and Casino, was built by the Cornero brothers in early 1931 after legal gambling returned to Nevada. Tony and Frank Cornero were big bootleggers and built their establishment just outside city limits near Fremont and Charleston, along busy Boulder Highway. It was the first resort hotel in the Las Vegas area. It opened in

Undated photo of Tony Cornero
Courtesy of the Nevada State Museum, Las Vegas

May of 1931 and hoped to serve dam workers as well as tourists. Designed to have a hotel with 25 rooms, it also offered music, prohibited fine whiskey, dancing, food, a pool and gambling. The casino was allowed to have two crap tables, two roulette tables, two blackjack tables, a faro table, a Big Six Wheel and five slot machines. A small airplane landing strip was cleared adjacent to the resort. Visitors to the property came in their finest garb to enjoy fine dining and an evening of entertainment.

A July 6, 1931, photo of the Meadows
Courtesy of the Nevada State Museum, Las Vegas

July 2, 1931, Las Vegas Age
entertainment ad for the Meadows

July 1931 photo of folks enjoying gambling in the Meadow's casino. Tony Cornero is the man seated in the lower left corner of the photo.
*UNLV Libraries, Special Collections;
Dokter Photo Collection (0012 0144)*

About four months after opening, a fire damaged the hotel section of the Meadows. The Cornero's were upset that the Las Vegas Fire Department failed to show up to fight the fire as their resort was just outside city limits. After repairs were made, they sold the hotel portion of the resort to none other than Alex Richmond. Richmond now had his long-desired hotel resort, even though less spectacular than what he originally dreamed of years earlier. Richmond would lease the hotel out for a few years before selling it in 1935. The new owners let it fall into disrepair and it became a known location for prostitution. Federal officials forced it to close in 1942 as it was too close to the Army Air Corps Gunnery base and its personnel. A year later the Meadows was destroyed by fire. (Alex Richmond passed away in 1952.)

The saga of early large Las Vegas hotel projects does not end with the Meadows. In April of 1931 Leigh Hunt resurfaced with a $750,000 200-room hotel project to be built at Fremont and 7th Street. His timing

Employees pose for this photo taken outside the Meadows after the fire of 1931
UNLV Libraries, Special Collections;
Elton & Madelaine Garret Photo Collection (0265 0190)]

was poor as the Great Depression was deepening. When his old Cleveland investors came to discuss the project, they were hit by a vicious Las Vegas dust storm which had them back out once again. Hunt surrendered. He was done. He would die a little over two years later.

Finally, there would be a group of men with Palm Springs hotel ties in 1936 headed by San Diego broker Harry Wiesler (age 39) that wanted to build an 880-acre $2.5 million hotel called "El Sonador" ("The Dream" of the Desert). It was to be on the land where the current incomplete Fontainebleau/Drew Hotel project sits today on Las Vegas Blvd. It was to have 100 to 150 rooms (including private guest cottages), a casino, a spa, outdoor dining patio, tennis courts, a pool, a golf course, a large fountain and a winter racetrack with stables. Wiesler produced a 17-page prospectus (which the railroad called a "promotional scheme"). After struggling to secure financial backing (he could only line up $280,000 of the needed $600,000) and with the railroad denying him a substantial supply of water, he finally gave up.

It would not be until April of 1941 when the first long-lasting hotel resort appeared. The "El Rancho Vegas" opened with 66 rooms on Highway 91 and became a model for future hotel projects that followed.

One of the principal reasons why most of the early resort projects failed was because the railroad failed to invest funds. They felt comfortable offering land but not money nor water. Also the First State Bank wanted no part of the projects. Outside financial backing was weak and Las Vegas lacked a sufficient number of well-to-do residents who could afford to make sizeable stock purchases in the projects. Wildly varying changes in projected construction costs also did not help.

So there you have it. A gold mine that looked very real, ranch land and housing projects that seemed so promising, and proposed hotel resorts that resulted in numerous huge disappointments. Were they just scams, schemes and broken dreams or just a bunch of unachievable "air projects" brought forth by men with desire and incredible vision?

About the Author

Author Jeff Alpert was born and raised in Brooklyn, New York in 1952. He moved at age 13 with his family to Los Angeles where he attended local secondary schools. Jeff majored in mathematics at U.C.L.A. and earned his Master's Degree in the Teaching of Mathematics in 1976. He went on to teach middle school math for 30 years with the Los Angeles Unified School District. After retirement, he decided to move to North Las Vegas, Nevada to enjoy a quieter and less stressful life.

Jeff remains very active in his community. He serves on the Citizens Advisory Committee in North Las Vegas and is also a director of a local citizen's group. Jeff also is a homeowner association president. He is an active participant in many local "friends" support groups.

The author hopes that all three of his self-published books increase the public's interest in local history. For his first two books, profits from sales were directed to the Friends of the North Las Vegas Libraries. The profits from this book will be going to the Friends of the Nevada State Museum in Las Vegas.